<u>First President and Father of the Nation, Tanzania</u>

MWALIMU JULIUS KAMBARAGE NYERERE'S VISION OF EDUCATION

Juvenalis Rwelamira Paulo Baitu

- Catholic Priest,
- PhD in Moral Theology,
- Professor, Social Political Ethics,
- Formerly Professor at the Catholic University of Eastern Africa.
- Currently Deputy Principal Administration and Finance at The Cardinal Rugambwa Memorial College, Bukoba Tanzania.

TANZANIA EDUCATIONAL PUBLISHERS LTD

Tanzania Educational Publishers Ltd,
TEPU House,
Uganda Road,
Plot No. 45, Block MDA,
Telephone: 0685997583/0758147871
Email: tepultd@yahoo.com
Website: www.tepu.co.tz
P.O.Box. 1222,
Bukoba, Tanzania.

Mobiles: +255 758 040 661

Email: jrbaitu@yahoo.com

ISBN 978 9987 07 080 0

Dedication

To the people of Tanzania
in search for their sustainable development

Table of Contents

Acknowledgements

It is an esteemed custom and practice of the traditional African people within their *Ujamaa* (extended family members) context to express their gratitude for a gift and support offered to them.

Therefore, within the same context and sentiment, it is a noble and humble duty to acknowledge the wisdom of the many people without which this work could be brought to its fruitful completion. I am aware of the fact that I may not recall all those eminent people who have contributed, in different ways to this work. This does not mean that I underrate the significance of their generosity. I fully and humbly express my appreciation for their support.

First and foremost, I acknowledge the Chairman of the Council and the Vice Chancellor of the Catholic University of Eastern Africa for granting me the sabbatical year for this research work. I acknowledge my Bishop, Rt. Rev. Desiderius Rwoma for the permission he gave me to conduct my research; Rt. Rev. Method Kilaini for his continuous friendship and encouragement and the Most Rev. Novatus Rugambwa, Apostolic Nuncio, for his moral and material support. I recognize in a special way the hospitality and generosity I received from the Archdiocese of Dar es Salaam, His Eminence Polycarp Cardinal Pengo and his Auxiliary, Rt. Rev. Eusebius Nzigilwa for accommodating me, assuring me all the spiritual, moral and material support I needed for research and publication of this work. To the Parish Priest, Rev. Dr. Joseph Matumaini, all the clergy, religious and laity of St. Jospeh's Cathedral Parish, Archdiocese of Dar es Salaam deserve my special thanks for their generosity during the time we have prayed and celebrated life together. May they receive God's choicest blessing.

May I now in a special way acknowledge the resourcefulness of Thomas Molony, (2014). His detailed presentation and open discussion of the early years of Mwalimu Julius Kambarage Nyerere has served as the main source of chapter one of this work. I can't appreciate enough the assistance I received from the Executive Director, Mr. Joseph Butiku, his deputy, Mr. Gallus Abedi, for generously availing me with all the relevant written resources, and oral information coupled with regular discussions on my research topic; the staff, and the office space at the Mwalimu Nyerere Foundation (Taasisi ya Mwalimu Nyerere), Dar es Salaam. May the Almighty God bless them with good health and wisdom to contribute to the prosperity of the Foundation within the Mwalimu Nyerere's intended objectives. Their support has enabled me to bring this work to its successful completion.

I also extend my gratitude to the many prominent academicians, socio-political scientists, philosophers, theologians and religious leaders for their precious ideas as acknowledged in the footnotes all through the text and the list of the main references. I acknowledge and fully own errors, if any, on account of my limited interpretation, which was, of course, not intended.

Finally, my sincere thanks extends to all the benefactors, both individuals as well as my brother priests, sisters of religious communities and the laity in the Archdiocese of Dar es Salaam and the Catholic Diocese of Bukoba; to my family, my friends at the Catholic University of Eastern Africa, Nairobi and all over, for their constant prayers, encouragement, moral and material support which made my sabbatical year of research and writing enjoyable and fruitful.

Juvenalis Paul Baitu Rwelamira

Dar es Salaam, Tanzania

25th February, 2019.

Preface

This small book is about Mwalimu Julius K. Nyerere. It has been written by Prof. Baitu. He knew Mwalimu Nyerere, and who he was, but also he had a passionate desire to share with others, especially those who will read this book, the philosophy, principles and beliefs that made Mwalimu Nyerere he writes about, and the one admired by many more people inside and outside Tanzania.

Mwalimu Nyerere was a philosopher; but how many people now understand and accept that philosophy, leave alone whether they are able to share a belief with Mwalimu in that philosophy? Mwalimu Nyerere was highly principled man, and a staunch believer in the world, and in the history of mankind. And who, like him, who has ever associated his belief in the World and history. How many of us are able to give a correct interpretation of all that today, while Mwalimu Nyerere himself, is no longer with us? But he has widely written about himself, and humanity as a whole – he taught us about the different, and not so obvious truth that *"Binadamu wote ni ndugu zangu"* – a literal translation would probably read: all people are my brothers and sisters.

But Mwalimu Nyerere left us with a legacy – a heritage of good leadership rooted in the values he believed in; the equality of all men and women without discrimination, respect for humanity, freedom for all – individuals and groups, democracy (the right for all individuals and groups to participate in all decisions relating to their well-being). All this is what Mwalimu Nyerere referred to as 'UJAMAA' – Familyhood. May be you have never stopped to think seriously and deeply about the genesis of all that you may be admiring about Mwalimu. To some people, Mwalimu is their role-model! But why? The answer lies in you deciding to read this small book.

In Chapter two of this small book the author argues that

"Nyerere always had an ideal society (Tanganyika) in his mind based on human equality, freedom and unity of all Tanganyikans".

Handing a copy of my published book to Mwalimu Nyerere, at St. Egidio Community International Centre in Rome, Italy, March 1988.

To Mwalimu these, together with two others – democracy and the necessity for work by all, are the pillars of any viable nation state. These are the pillars upon which Nyerere built Tanganyika, and later Tanzania Nation. The author's views fully support Mwalimu's actual basis of the ideal society he was talking about, and upon which he had a vision to build the type of country he wanted, and the kind of Africa and the world generally he would wish to live in! This is what he says:

"Thus the ideal society is based on human equality and on a combination of the freedom and unity of its members. There must be equality, because only on that basis will men work, cooperatively. There must be freedom, because the individual is not served by society unless it is his. And there must be unity because only when the society is united can its members live and work in peace, security and well-being.... The essential nature of these requirements, and their implications, can be seen most easily in the smallest sound unit and the one which was in its time perhaps the most satisfactory to its members- the traditional African family."

The discourse in this small book is basically about what is quoted above. I recommend this book be treated as a "must-read" for all those who have an honest interest in Mwalimu Nyerere, and what he stood for. The book is small, and written in simple language, yet it is beautiful, most interesting and generously informative and educative.

I thank and congratulate Professor Baitu for writing it and for the courage of making it available to the general public.

Joseph W. Butiku
Executive Director
THE MWALIMU NYERERE FOUNDATION

Abbreviations

ESR	Education for Self-Reliance
TDV	Tanzania Development Vision
TAWA	Tanganyika African Welfare Association
CDWS	Colonial Development and Welfare Scheme
CAF	Central African Federation
TANU	Tanganyika African National Union
TASWA	Tanganyika African Students Association
MNF	The Mwalimu Nyerere Foundation

Introduction

Mwalimu Julius Kambarage Nyerere was an intellectual, scholar, and a teacher. He articulated his beliefs and principles. He eloquently shared them in a clear and simple way that could be easily understood by all people regardless of their tribe, race, gender, political affiliation, religion, young and old; intellectuals as well as those who never went through formal education. He was consistent, committed, courageous and persuasive in expressing his views, both in word and actions as his personal contribution to the people-centered development of all Tanzanians and the people of Africa. Indeed he was a teacher whose words, personal practices and writings continue to communicate practical meaning long after his death.

His vision of education gradually developed throughout his formative years as he contemplated on the purpose of education everywhere in the world and more so in the developing nation like Tanzania. All through his presidential leadership tenure in Tanzania, Mwalimu Nyerere labored through his speeches, writings and action-oriented meetings, seminars, public debates and workshops to promote people-centered development activities. His vision of education officially articulated in his policy document, 'Education for Self-Reliance' (ESR) at the heart of the Arusha Declaration (1967) remains a key source for the meaning and purpose of education in Tanzania in search of sustainable development.

This work, therefore, is an attempt to stir the debate among the Tanzanians educators and education activists, strategic development planners, Ministry of Education and relevant Government ministries, stakeholders in the provision of education (public and private), politicians, business communities, parents and guardians, all Tanzanians of good will, regarding the perennial value of Mwalimu Nyerere's vision of education articulated in his policy document 'Education for Self-Reliance' (ESR); and its relevance and potential for the realization of Tanzania Development Vision (TDV) 2025.

This work consists of five chapters. Chapter One explores, in a nutshell, who Mwalimu Julius Kambarage Nyerere is and the contribution of his commitment to Christian-Catholic faith his life-style and presidential leadership tenure. Chapter Two discusses the Tanzanian Society Mwalimu Nyerere Envisaged. Chapter Three examines Mwalimu Nyerere's Vision of Education. It points out the implantation of his vision and the challenges it encountered within the context of *Ujamaa* life setting of early 1960s and late 1970s; and the liberal capitalistic setting of early 1980s to date. Chapter Four revisit Mwalimu

Nyerere's view of Education within Tanzania todate. Chapter Five proposes deliberate actions to be taken in the process of revisiting Mwalimu Nyerere's Vision of Education and its successful application today and the future of Tanzania.

It concludes with an imperative that calls all leaders of Tanzanians to emulate Mwalimu Nyerere, who is well-recognize - by the absolute majority of Tanzanians - as *'Baba wa Taifa'*; a living example. In doing so, become practitioners whose lives demonstrate the reality that the values and principles described earlier on, are worthy pursuing and abiding by, for workable daily engagement in their noble tasks for sustainable development.

1
CHAPTER

MWALIMU JULIUS KAMBARAGE NYERERE

Julius Kambarage Nyerere was born on 13 April 1922 in Mwitongo into the Zanaki tribe of Butiama, a rural village in North-Western Tanzania, near the east cost of Lake Victoria. His father was Chief Nyerere Burito and his mother was Mugaya Nyang'ombe, baptized Christina Mugaya in her mid-seventies.[1]

Mama Mugaya Nyang'ombe, Mwalimu Nyerere's mother.
She was born 1892 and died on 5th September, 1997
(Source: MNF Archive).

---

[1] Cf. Thomas Molony, Nyerere: The Early Years, Woodbridge, Suffolk, 2014, p. 35.

His very earliest years were certainly not very much different from his age - mates in Butiama village. As Molony notes, "he was helping farming of the millet, maize, and cassava. He was barefoot and often ate only one meal a day [..]. As with other young boys, they would herd goats together, and latter, cattle."[2] Nyerere was the son of a chief, yet he himself recalled that "he was trying to sleep under a leaky roof at home, and that there was not always adequate food for what was often the family's single daily meal."[3] This is indicative of the fact that although he was a son of a chief he did not enjoy the benefits of his status as it could have been compared to the sons of chiefs throughout Tanganyika of that time. Living within a community of his father's twenty two wives gave him an opportunity to experience community life that would influence his later leadership.[4]

Kambarage Nyerere acknowledged the key role his mother and father played on the early stages of his life; a thing that was common to other young Zanaki boys of Butiama. Nevertheless, as a son of a chief, growing in a chief's household, his upbringing was relatively privileged than that of other children in Uzanaki."[5]

Kambarage Nyerere begun his formal education in February 1934 at Mwisenge Native Administration School, Musoma.[6] 'On 20 April, 1934, a week after his twelfth birthday, Kambarage enrolled in Standard I at Mwisenge Native Authority School, given the registration number 308.[7]

---

[2] Ibid., pp.38-39.
[3] Ibid., p.39.
[4] Ibid.
[5] Ibid., pp.41-43.
[6] Ibid., p.43; see also Nyerere, J.K. 'Uhuru wa Wanawake' notebook, Mwalimu Nyerere Foundation/Taasisi ya Mwalimu Nyerere, Dar es Salaam.
[7] Ibid.., p.47; see Kitundu, S. 'Reflections:3, in Tanzania Standard, ed. Nyerere: 1961-1985 – Passing on the tongs, Dar es Salaam: Tanzania Standard, 1986, pp.47-48.

At school, Kambarage Nyerere excelled in arithmetic and other subjects.[8] 'In the examination that Kambarage and Kitundu did after six months, they performed so well that they were allowed to skip Standard II and moved to Standard III'.[9] Apart from his academic excellence, Kambarage had 'innate ability to be a role model for other pupils; he was not arrogant, like other children of chiefs, and was respectful to his fellows as well as teachers.'[10] Meanwhile, Kambarage started attending Roma Catholic instruction classes under the White Fathers/Missionaries of Africa, as his first exposure to Christianity.[11]

'Kambarage completed his primary school at Mwisenge in 1936; becoming 'top in the highly selective territorial examination'.12 In the following year, having received a government scholarship, and passing through a competitive process, was admitted at Tabora Government School/Tabora boys, an English public school in Africa, the school of the sons of chiefs.13 At Tabora boys, sports was still not one of his interests; he became a Patrol Leader of Rover Scout in the Boys Scouts, yet remaining a studious pupil, comfortable in his own company, but setting aside time for debating in the English Debating Society.[14]

Kambarage's father, Chief Nyerere Burito died in March 1942, during his final year at Tabora. Seven months after his father's funeral in Mwitongo, Kambarage completed his secondary school studies and returned home to Butiama.[15] Shortly after his return home, Kambarage went to Nyengina Mission, eight miles, from Musoma to speak with Father Matthias Konen, Missionaries of

---

[8] Kitundu, 'Reflections', p.47.
[9] Molony, ibid.., p.46.
[10]Kitundu, 'Reflections', p.47.
[11]Molony, pp.48-50.
[12]Molony, p.53.
[13]Ibid., pp.53-54.
[14] Ibid., pp.55-58.
[15] Ibid., p.61.

Africa, and requested for baptism.[16] Kambarage was to undergo special catechetical classes given by Petro Maswe Marwa, a catechist in preparation for baptism.[17]

In November, 1942 Kambarage sat for Uganda's Makerere College entrance examination. He obtained a bursary from Tabora Boys to do a teacher training course at Makerere the following year.[18] On 23 December 1942, Kambarage was baptized a Roman Catholic, Julius Kambarage Nyerere, in Nyegina Catholic Mission, by Father Aloysius Junker, a White Father; his former catechist, Petro Maswe Marwa was his godfather.[19]

In January 1943, at the age of twenty two, Julius Kambarage Nyerere left his country for Makerere College Uganda. Makerere College introduced Julius Kambarage Nyerere to a new world of the brilliant young men of Tanganyika's nobility with the purpose of furthering their education and building a solid foundation for illustrious career.[20] Julius devoted his time to his studies; very soon he gained a reputation in debating in the Makerere Debating Society. Furthermore, he gradually developed a political stance as expressed in his article, entitled African Socialism, written on 10 July 1943; only six months at Makerere published in the Tanganyika Standard, in which he argued that capitalism is alien to African society. The article testified to his independent intellectual growth, and marked the beginning of Julius Kambarage Nyerere's political maturation already at his teenage stage.[21]

On religious matters, Julius Kambarage Nyerere read and studied the Papal Encyclicals to deepen his Christian faith and Catholic life in the family and society.

---

[16] Ibid., pp.62-63.
[17] Willie, 'Recollections', p.4.
[18] Molony, p.63.
[19] Ibid, p.63.
[20] Ibid., pp.65-66.
[21] Ibid., pp.65-72.

Moreover, he founded a branch of Catholic Action, whose focus is the participation of the laity in the apostolate of defending religious and moral principles for the development of wholesome and beneficent social action in the restoration of Catholic life in the family and society.[22] Julius Kambarage Nyerere received the Sacrament of Confirmation on 30 May 1944 at Rubaga Mission, Kampala- Uganda.[23]

Julius Kambarage Nyerere pioneered in forming the non-political Tanganyika African Welfare Association (TAWA), and drafting its constitution. The main purpose of the Association was to improve the lives of the fellow Tanganyika Students at Makerere. He served as secretary and later as chairman of the association.[24]

In 1945, Julius Kambarage Nyerere graduated from Makerere three-year teachers training course with a Teachers' Diploma.[25] He returned to Butiama, spent sometimes building a house for his mother, mix freely with people around the village, visit relatives, do farming with a hoe like ordinary people; while remaining as studious as ever.[26] In the course of his stay at Butiama, he received an offer for his first teaching job, as fully qualified teacher, at the Catholic St. Mary's School in Tabora from Fr. Richard Walsh, a White Father missionary, the Director of the School. Julius Nyerere accepted the offer and started his teaching job at the beginning of January 1946.[27] Shortly after being employed at St. Mary's, Julius Nyerere joined the recently-opened African Association branch in Tabora; he was elected Treasurer. A few months later, he traveled to the African Association's conference in Dar es Salaam, an opportunity that enabled him to meet the Association delegates from throughout

---

[22] Ibid., p.75.
[23] Ibid., pp.75-76; Willie, 'Recollections', p.4.
[24] Ibid.,p.76; see Tibandebage, 'Life', p.x.
[25] Ibid., pp.78-79; see NACO981/16556/20.
[26] Ibid., p.79, Interview, Jack Nyamwaga.
[27] Ibid., p.80.

Tanganyika for the first time. Moreover, it gave him an opportunity to know the important political issues concerning Tanganyika. It also gave him an opportunity to present a memorandum that 'formed the basis of a conference resolution demanding constitutional advance through a pyramid of elected councils'.[28] This marked his entry into territorial politics.[29]

While in Tabora, Nyerere continued to write articles for newspapers and magazines, as he did at Makerere.[30] The value of education and socio-economic responsibilities that it imposed on its recipients was the recurring theme throughout his writings and speeches.[31] These ideas formed the initial stages of his philosophy of education for self-reliance.

At St. Mary's, Nyerere was considering to marry Maria Waningu Magige, as well as undertaking higher education abroad.[32] Fr. Richard Walsh (White Fathers) registered him for the University of London Matriculation Examination. Nyerere was tested on English, Swahili, Elementary Mathematics, Biology and History of the British Empire. He passed with Second Class Division in January 1948.[33] Father Walsh succeeded in raising the funds for Nyerere's higher education, but he turned down the offer, most probably for his enduring motive of strengthening the unity of the Zanaki people and their chiefs; and the Tanganyika African Association that was vigorously growing in the Lake Province in 1948, with Mwanza in the process of becoming the association's National Headquarters.[34]

---

[28] Ibid., pp.81-82.

[29] Ibid., p.82; cf. Illiffe, Modern History, p.432.

[30] Ibid., p.85; cf. Tibandebage, in Mwakikagile, Nyerere, p.401.

[31] Ibid., pp.85-86; cf. Duggan, W.R., Civille, J.R. Tanzania and Nyerere: A Study of Ujamaa and Nationhood, Maryknoll, NY: Orbis, 1976, p.26; Nyerere to the editors of Makerere Magazine, November 1946, Vol. 1 No. 1, p.35; Also Hatch, African Statesmen, pp.24-25.

[32] Ibid., p.93.

[33] Ibid., p.93.

[34] Ibid., pp.93-96.

'Torn between home and abroad, Julius looked for advice from James Irenge, the self-deal breaker, who advised him to go for his studies in the United Kingdom'.[35] 'He decided to specialize in teaching, so that he could help more people'.[36] Thus he took the offer 'for a four-year scholarship awarded by the Colonial Development and Welfare Scheme (CDWS) for a science degree course to become a qualified science teacher'.[37]

Mwalimu Nyerere and his wife Maria with their family members at State House, Dar es Salaam (Source: MNF Archive)

Julius and Maria were informally engaged shortly before Christmas 1948, before his departure to Europe for higher education.[38] On the recommendation of Father Walsh, Maria

---

[35] Ibid., pp.96-97.
[36] Ibid., p.97; cf. Interview, Adam Marwa.
[37] Ibid., pp.96-97; cf. NACO981/16556/25-26.
[38] Ibid., pp.97-98; cf. Hatch, African Statesmen, p.24.

proceeded to Stella Maris College, in Nsube, Uganda to undertake her studies in Domestic Science. This was important to ensure there was less difference in formal education between Julius and Maria.[39] Despite the fact that the two had not entered a formal marriage, nonetheless, they agreed to remain faithful while abroad, far from one another.[40] In March 1949, Julius Nyerere wished goodbye to his trusted friends in Tabora, Oswald's family and Mama Magori in Nyigina, preparing himself for his travel to Europe.[41] "On Saturday 9 April 1949 Julius Nyerere boarded the British Overseas Airways in Dar es Salaam to England, [....], arriving in Southampton on 12 April 1949".[42]

Nyerere spent his first full day in Britain, on his 27th Birthday, in London. He lodged for a week at the Balmoral Hotel in Victoria. He had a series of meetings at the Colonial Office Headquarters discussing his degree course studies. On 20th April 1949 he boarded a train to Edinburgh Waverley Station where he was met by a member of the Colonial Office Welfare Department who accompanied him to the Colonial House, 2, Palmerston Road, University Residence for colonial students.[43]

Nyerere expressed his wish to study an Arts degree during his meeting with Colonial Office officials in London. Of the three options he was given, he preferred Edinburgh's Ordinary "Masters of Arts" (M.A. which took three years) for the main reason of being more useful to 'my country' [....] than a Science degree', a fact that he had seriously considered long before his Edinburgh studies.[44] 'In October 1949 he received good news that

---

[39] Ibid., p.98.
[40] Ibid., p.98.
[41] Ibid., pp.98-99.
[42] Ibid., pp.101-102.
[43] Ibid., pp.102-105.
[44] Ibid., pp.108-109.

he had been accepted for entry at the University of Edinburgh's Faculty of Arts to study for a Master of Arts degree'.[45]

Nyerere's Edinburgh studies showed an overall steady improvement from the first to the third and final year.[46] The choice of anthropological and philosophical courses he took during this time of study were made with the view of developing his basic orientation to becoming a person who would serve his country in whatever capacity as he had expressed long before his Edinburgh studies.[47]

While in Edinburgh, Nyerere informally assumed the role of communicating about activities with fellow Tanganyikan students in the United Kingdom and his former Makerere and Tabora friends at home.[48] He also took a prominent and active part in African politics with particular concern with the increasing 'white-domination over the emerging Central African Federation (CAF)'.[49]

Nevertheless, this engagement did not divert him from his primary focus on his studies. He spent time in discussion with his lecturers and tutors; and in writing manuscripts for journals drawing insights from the literature he was reading for his courses and other extracurricular books for his personal independent reading.[50] Nyerere developed his political philosophy from a wide range of the philosophers he studied in Edinburgh and his lecturers who guided him towards a reflective study of them[51] that

---

[45] Ibid.
[46] Ibid., pp.111-114.
[47] Ibid., pp.111-115.
[48] Ibid., pp.133-134.
[49] Ibid., pp. 137-143.
[50] Ibid., pp.143-162.
[51] Ibid., pp.147-162.

had great impact on his later political thought and full time engagement in politics.

Nyerere successfully completed his studies and graduated from Edinburgh with an Ordinary Degree of Masters of Arts on 4 July 1952.[52] On 7 October 1952 Nyerere took a flight from London (via Nairobi) and arrived in Dar es Salaam on 9 October 1952.[53] Shortly later he went to Butiama to reunite with his mother, Mugaya Nyang'ombe, Chief Edward Wanzagi, his half brother, Maria, his fiance'e, his old friends and Uzanaki elders.[54] On 21 January 1953, Julius Kambarage Nyerere and Maria Waningu Gabriel Magige were married in Musoma Roma Catholic Church. In February 1953, they moved to Pugu, at St. Francis College, on the outskirts of Dar es Salaam, where he was to begin his teaching job.[55] While at Pugu, Nyerere was soon absorbed in political activities of Tanganyika African Association whose headquarters was in Dar es Salaam, that gradually reshaped to Tanganyika African National Union (TANU) under Nyerere's leadership on 7 July 1954. Caught up in between teaching and political activities, the two of which he was devoted yet could not mix, Julius had to resign teaching at Pugu on 22 March 1955.[56]

Julius Kambarage Nyerere devoted his time and energy applying his knowledge to lead the people of Tanganyika to independence on 9 December 1961. In January 1962 he resigned as Prime Minister to lead TANU into a government institution. On 9

---

[52] Ibid., p.180; see Edinburgh University, University Calender: 1952-1953, Edinburgh: James Thin, p.705; Graduates in Arts, 1952, EUA INI/ADS/5, EUL.
[53] Ibid., p.183.
[54] Ibid., pp.184-188.
[55] Ibid., p.189.
[56] Ibid., p.193; see Interview, Nyamwaga; also Recollections on President Julius Kambarage Nyerere, Unpublished notes of Father Arthur H. Willie, M.M., Musoma, 1 February 2005, p.12.

December 1962 Julius Kambarage Nyerere was sworn in as the first President of the Republic of Tanganyika. In 1964 he worked for the unification of Tanganyika and Zanzibar to form Tanzania him becoming the first president. In 1985 he retired as the President of the United Republic of Tanzania. However, he remained as the Chairman of Chama Cha Mapinduzi (CCM) until 1990. He also served as Chairman of the International South Commission (1987-1990); and Chairman of the South Centre in Geneva and Dar es Salaam Offices (1990-1999). Julius Kambarage Nyerere died in a London hospital on 14 October 1999.[57]

---

[57] Library, Mwalimu Nyerere Foundation/Taasisi ya Mwalimu Nyerere, Dar es Salaam.

2
CHAPTER

MWALIMU JULIUS KAMBARAGE NYERERE: A DEVOUT CHRISTIAN

Mwalimu Julius Kambarage Nyerere's Roman Catholic faith had a remarkable influence on his personality, character, educational choices and the development of his political leadership style in the service of his fellow Tanzanians, the people of Africa and the world over regardless of their race, social status, political affiliation and religion.

As much as he trained as a teacher at Makerere College, Kampala, Uganda, he also studied Greek and Latin, which were later on instrumental in translating the Sunday Epistles and Gospels to the Zanaki language in aid of the Missionaries of Africa (White Fathers) for their apostolate in Zanaki land and to understand his faith well. Moreover, he studied the Papal Encyclicals and the Catholic philosophers to deepen the knowledge and nourish his growing Roman Catholic faith.[58]

Furthermore, he founded a branch of 'Catholic Action'; organized annual retreats and pilgrimages to the Uganda Martyrs' Shrine, Namugongo, Kampala, Uganda; and organized his fellow Tanganyikans to form the nucleus of a Welfare Association whose aim was to improve the lives of the Tanganyika students at Makerere University College, Kampala.[59]

---

[58]Father Arthur H. Willie, M.M., *Recollections on President Julius Kambarage Nyerere*, Unpublished notes, 1 February 2005, p.4.
[59]Idem, p.4.

While at Edinburgh, Mwalimu Nyerere kept his faith commitment profound and personal. He may have 'spent time in prayer or reflecting, and attending Mass at the Chaplaincy at 23, George Square; likely joined the Catholic Students' Union; and at some point contemplated priestly vocation in the Catholic Church, so that he could serve God and do a lot of good to people'.[60]

Mwalimu Nyerere had to resign from teaching so that he could devote more time to serve the Tanganyikans through Tanganyika African Union (TANU), a political party that lead Tanganyika (Tanzania Mainland) to independence. Back home to Butiama with is family, he taught Fr. Willie the Zanaki language; translated from Kwaya language into Zanaki language the two catechisms and a hymnal that the Missionaries of Africa had composed to help the catechists to teach the catechumens. Moreover, Julius would help the missionaries in translating what the Zanaki had to say to them as they were undertaking their pastoral ministry.[61]

During the campaigns for independence, Julius sacrificed his salary to support TANU's activities. As President of TANU, he travelled around the country talking about the fundamental values of: hard work, mutual respect, equality in every respect for all people, non-discrimination on the basis of tribe, race, or religion. His focus was on a greater task of fighting poverty, ignorance and disease.[62]

His day always begun with participating in the Holy Mass and receiving Holy Communion at St. Peter's Parish, Oysterbay in Dar es Salaam, Tanzania, or elsewhere in different parts of Tanzania where he would be on his presidential duties. While

---

[60]Molony, Idem, pp.175-177.
[61]Idem, *Recollections*, pp.7-10.
[62]Idem, pp.11-16.

abroad, his aides would locate the Catholic Church and the time for the celebration of the Holy Mass that he could worship God and receive Holy Communion. For example, when he went to Dakar, Senegal on State visit, Julius K. Nyerere requested his host, President Leopord Senghor to invite a priest to the State House to celebrate the Holy Mass for them. The arrangement was made; a priest came and celebrated the Holy Mass for them.[63]

Mwalimu Julius K. Nyerere (in Kaunda Suit) joined with his family sharing a light moment with Pope John Paul II during Pope's official visit to Tanzania in September, 1990 (Source: MNF Archive).

The reason he gave for his practice is that he 'believed that it is God who entrusted him with the responsibility to lead His people; therefore he had to begin his working day with God's guidance and inspiration; he had also to ask for forgiveness for his service's imperfections; and had to entrust the people he was leading to

---

[63]Peter D.M. Bwimbo, *Mlinzi Mkuu wa Mwalimu Nyerere*, Dar es Salaam, Mkuki na Nyota Publishers, 2016, pp.37-38.

God their Creator'.[64] He regularly received the Sacrament of Reconciliation.[65]

Mwalimu Julius Kambarage Nyerere wrote the poetic version of the Four Gospels and the Acts of the Apostles into Kiswahili language.[66]He had special devotion to the Blessed Mother Mary, Our Lady of Grace, of whose Statue he had wanted to erect a shrine among the granite rocks near his burial place in Butiama. While in Butiama, he would gather his grandchildren to teach them Roman Catholic prayers. He raised money from his Canadian friends and with the help of Tanzanian Catholic Bishops to build a Church in Butiama where he could go for the daily Holy Mass and receive Holy Communion.[67] He respected other people's religious beliefs and encouraged the Tanzanians to do the same.

The 24 years of Mwalimu Julius Kambarage Nyerere's total dedication in the service of the Tanzanians and the people of other nations[68] were faced with successes and challenges. He faithfully kept his principles of non-discrimination on the basis of tribe, race, social status and religion. He served to ensure the respect of human dignity and equity in the distribution of goods and services so that all Tanzanians could work together in their search for sustainable solutions to poverty, ignorance and disease.

---

[64]Testimony of Joseph Butiku and Gallus Abedi, Interviewees, 5 January 2018.
[65]Idem.
[66]Julius K.Nyerere, *Injili na Matendo ya Mitume*, Ndanda-Peramiho, Benedictine Publications, 1966.
[67]Idem, *Recollections*, p.17.
[68]Mwalimu Nyerere served as Chairman of the International South Commission, 1987-1990; Chairman of the South Centre in Geneva and Dar es Salaam, 1990-1999; Chief Mediator in the Burundi Conflict, 1996.

On account of his humility, simplicity and magnanimity he wanted no privileges for him and his family, but to live and be with the majority of the people of Tanzania. Concretely, he refused the title of "Mtukufu" (The Honorable/His Excellency) and preferred the title "Mwalimu" (Teacher); he lowered his salary by ten percent. Likewise, other senior government employees' salaries were reduced at the same or lower percentage. The main objective was to minimize the difference in income that existed between the highly and lowest paid Tanzanian employees.[69]

He categorically rejected the idea of erecting his statue at Azikiwe-Samora streets junction in the heart of Dar es Salaam city, to replace that of the Askari (war soldier).[70]He rejected extraordinary security around him and his family. Furthermore, he rejected big presidential motorcade and siren for the sole reason that it was a nuisance, disturbing and depriving the drivers their rights of roads; and become source of unnecessary road accidents and delays to their work stations.[71]

He would spend his vacation in Butiama with the people in his neighbourhood; work together with them in his farm, planting crops, weeding, harvesting, and sharing meals with them.[72]He was honest, truthful, just and responsible; thus fought all forms of corruption, himself leading by example of not engaging in corrupt deals even when in doing so it would cost the country foreign aid.[73]

---

[69]Peter D.M. Bwimbo, pp.55-58.
[70]Idem, pp.60-61.
[71]Idem, pp.31-32, 62-64.
[72]Idem, pp.32-33; Idem, *Recollections*, p.17.
[73]Idem, *Recollections*, p.17; Peter D.M. Bwambo, pp.39-40, 52-57, 60-61; Mwalimu Julius Kambarage Nyerere, *Africa Today and Tomorrow*, Dar es Salaam, Mwalimu Nyerere Foundation, 2000, pp.22-24.

Mwalimu Nyerere was merciful and compassionate in dealing with others, although sometimes he would detain dissenters for some time and release them when the time was reasonably convenient. The good examples are: forgiving the Tanganyikan Rifles soldiers who lead the mutiny activities of January 1964; forgiving those who attempted to overthrow the government in 1968 and 1984;[74] applying his presidential right of prerogative of mercy to relieve the many individuals who were awaiting their death sentence and the lucky ones freed from prison when he officially submitted his retirement in 1985.[75]

As a human being he made mistakes together with his government all through the 24 years of his leadership. As he put it: "None of us is perfect. We cannot always see the full implications of what we do or say; and however much we try, none of us always resists the temptations and arrogance of office."[76] On this account he was always willing to admit the mistakes and change the policies to correct them for the common good of Tanzanians, especially the less fortunate of the masses of rural peasant farmers.

Most of the challenges and his government faced during the 24 years were related with the implementation of the 1967 Arusha Declaration regarding the nationalization of schools to ensure access by all Tanzanians to primary education regardless of their tribe, religion, social status; and major means of ownership and economic activities to fight exploitation and ensure equality in economic activity engagement and equitable distribution of goods and services. The villagilization policy was another challenge.

---

[74]Peter D.M. Bwimbo, pp.86-87; p.103.
[75]Idem, pp.37; 103; *Hotuba ya Rais Julius K. Nyerere Katika Bunge*, Dar es Salaam, 29 July 1985.
[76]Mwalimu Julius K. Nyerere, *Africa Today and Tomorrow*, Dar es Salaam, 2000, p.24.

With time some of the major policies related to the above were modified or dropped out so that the intended objectives of the people-centered development could gradually be achieved. The Kagera war with Iddi Amin troops of Uganda was another challenge.[77]

In a nutshell, Mwalimu Julius Kambarage Nyerere 'believed in the equality of all human beings and the duty to serve their well-being as well as their freedom and welfare as individuals and communities in their fellowship wherever they may be'[78] This is the belief he cherished, constantly articulated in simple and logical style, and urged all Tanzanians to embrace throughout his 24 years presidential tenure.

Mwalimu Julius Kambarage Nyerere's Roman Catholic faith commitment remained the sustaining inspiration in keeping his leadership principles, aimed at loving God and the Tanzanians; and other people in Africa and beyond. The Christian virtues of faith, hope, charity, prayer, justice, humility, repentance, honesty, patience, forgiveness, renunciation, dutifulness, among many others, remained indisputable sources of his personality and leadership style.

---

[77]For a detailed account regarding these and many other challenges, see *Hotuba ya Rais Julius K.Nyerere Katika Bunge*, Dar es Salaam, 29 July 1985.

[78]Mwalimu Julius K .Nyerere, *Africa Today and Tomorrow*, pp.23-24.

3
CHAPTER

THE TANZANIAN SOCIETY MWALIMU NYERERE ENVISAGED

Julius Kambarage Nyerere's formative years envisaged the type of nation he wanted to dedicate his life, professional and leadership energy. Right from his formative years he had a desire to improve the lives of others; Tanganyikans (later Tanzanians) as well as others in Africa and beyond. He gradually carried this motive all through his studies and later on during his political leadership tenure.

Julius Kambarage Nyerere's early life experiences seem to have influenced his attitude and actions of his later life. He grew up in a Zanaki village of basic rural equality common to rural Tanganyika; sleeping under a leaky roof at home; not always having adequate food for a single daily meal; living in a close proximity with his father's twenty-two wives.[79] Right from his childhood he was used to helping in the farming of millet, maize and cassava; herding cattle, goats and sheep; and hunting despite the fact that he was the son of a chief, of course with somehow a relatively privileged status. These experiences must have laid a strong foundation on which Julius Kambarage Nyerere developed his vision of the Tanganyika (later Tanzania) was built long before his formal education in Mwisenge, Musoma; Tabora; Makerere; and Edinburgh.[80]

---

[79] Molony, pp.38-39; reference to what Nyerere said regarding his childhood.
[80] Ibid.., pp.40-41.

Julius Kambarage Nyerere's schooling at Mwisenge, Musoma, built his reading and reflecting charisma, yet he would still help his mother and herd goats and cattle, teach his peer friends to read and write, 'signs pointing to Nyerere as teacher in the making'[81] The Tabora Boys schooling years were an opportunity of Julius Nyerere to improve his English by reading as much as possible; to develop his leadership and debating skills through Scouting for Boys and English Debating Society; serving as House Prefect; above all, developing his sense of justice through various interventions in the defense of the less privileged fellow pupils.[82] These opportunities groomed his aptitude for oration and persuasion, together with leadership skills he was to use later on in articulating the vision he had for an independent Tanganyika/Tanzania.

Makerere College introduced Nyerere to an even wider perspective of experiences and opportunities that would shape his future political leadership of the Tanganyika/Tanzania he had in mind. This is manifested in his 'article published in the *Tanganyika Standard* only six months into his time at Makerere signed off by 'JUKENYE' of July 10, 1943, in which he is discussing African Socialism'; calling on his fellow educated Africans to guiding their fellows towards a positive future of Tanganyika'.[83] Likewise, his essay on 'Uhuru wa Wanawake' of 1944, expressed his views on the freedom of women and their full equality with men.[84] Moreover, Nyerere founded a branch of 'Catholic Action' for the defense of religious and moral principles, and for the development of a wholesome and beneficent social action; for the restoration of Catholic life in the

---

[81] Ibid.., p.53.
[82] Ibid.., pp.56-57.
[83] Ibid.., pp.68-72.
[84] Ibid.., p.73.

family and society.[85] Nyerere was instrumental in the formation of the Tanganyika African Student Welfare Association (TASWA), Makerere University branch to assist the Tanganyikan students at the University College.[86]

Furthermore, the courses he took at the University of Edinburgh for a Master of Arts degree, (namely Political Economy, Social Anthropology, History, Moral Philosophy, and English Literature) were carefully chosen in view of forming his ability, basic orientation and life view for their future application in the service of the Tanganyikans.[87]

Nyerere had an ideal society (Tanganyika) based on human equality, freedom and unity of all Tanganyikans.[88] He had in mind a Tanganyika/Tanzania in 'which all her citizens are equal; where there is no division between the rulers and ruled; rich and poor'.[89] 'Freedom – the ability of Tanganyikans to determine their own future; freedom from hunger, disease, and poverty; freedom for the individual right to live in dignity and equality with others, right to freedom of speech, freedom to participate in the making of all decisions which affect his life; freedom to pursue his interest and inclinations'.[90] The Tanganyika that Nyerere had in mind was to develop as a 'direct extension of the traditional African family; a society where each member enjoyed a sufficient share of the primary material needs, namely food, shelter, health, education and work'.[91]

---

[85] Ibid.., pp.68-77.

[86] Ibid.., p.76.

[87] Ibid.., pp.108-115.

[88] Nyerere, *Freedom and Unity*, p.8.

[89] Molony, p.156; see Nyerere, 1961 *Presidential Inaugural Address*.

[90] Idem, Introduction to *Freedom and Unity*, p.7; see Molony, p.157.

[91] Molony, pp.159-161.

At his return from Edinburgh, Nyerere continued to develop his ideas in the period immediately before independence and many years after, culminating in the Arusha Declaration of 1967.[92] Nyerere envisaged a Tanganyika 'where each member of the family recognized the place and the rights of the other members'[93]; each person helps others and is helped by them in turn, drawing from the traditional African society traits to inform and form the wider Tanganyika society he dreamed of. The key tenets of the traditional African society (as he understood them from his Zanaki societal experience) would become essential characteristics of cooperation in the socio-political and economic organization of the Tanganyika he wanted to contribute in its building.[94]

The Tanganyika/Tanzania he had in mind would develop on the foundation of equal consideration of her citizens, democratic participation and sustainable development through self-reliance. Such a society would shift from norms encouraging acquisitiveness and self-seeking towards those favoring cooperation and collective advancement. This society would be based on customs and practices which bear an African traditional idea of mutual involvement in the family.

Nyerere describes this context of family hood as follows: "Both the "rich" and the "poor" individual were completely secure in African society. Natural catastrophe brought famine to everybody "poor" or "rich". Nobody starved, either of food or human dignity, because he(she) lacked personal wealth; he(she) could

---

[92]Ibid.., p.162.
[93]Idem, *Socialism and Rural Development*, 1968, p.338.
[94]Ibid.., *Socialism and Rural Development*, p.339.

depend on the wealth possessed by the community of which he(she) was a member'.[95]

Mwalimu Nyerere was convinced that the Tanzanians would develop on the foundation of their past and in the way which suits their needs. He says: "We are not importing a foreign ideology into Tanzania and trying to smoother our distinct social pattern with it. We are deliberately decided to grow a society, out of our own roots, but in a particular direction towards a particular kind of objective. We are doing this by emphasizing certain characteristics of our traditional organization, and extending them so that they can embrace the possibilities of modern technology and enable us to meet the challenge of life in the twentieth century world."[96]

The Tanzanian society he envisaged would be a society where people cared for each other's well-being. The differences of talents, possessions and services were basically needed to serve this fundamental objective. It is on this ground that the institutions and organizations therein could maintain their relevance and realize their true purpose.[97]

Such a society would cherish the human equality that goes beyond the tribe, community, religion, the nation, the continent, to the entire human society. All people are regarded as brothers and sisters–members of the ever extending family.[98]On this

---

[95] J.K.Nyerere, *Ujamaa: Essays on Socialism*, Dar es Salaam: Oxford University Press, 1968, pp.3-4; Juvenalis Baitu Rwelamira, *Tanzanian Socialism-Ujamaa and Gaudium et Spes: Two Convergent Designs of Integral Human Development*, Roma, 1988, p.5.
[96]Idem, *Freedom and Socialism/Uhuru na Ujamaa*, Dar es Salaam: Oxford University Press, 1968, p.2.
[97] Idem, *Ujamaa: Essays on Socialism*, p.11.
[98] Ibid.., pp.11-12.

account, the wealth that exists therein has to be used for the well-being of all citizens, each according to his or her needs.[99]

The Tanzanian society would gradually grow to becoming the society he was committed to develop. It would achieve her sustainable development by the gradual conversion of the people's attitude and the existing institutions.[100]Therefore, the development of the envisaged Tanzania would be achieved through the determination of the Tanzanians' needs and taking the direction that is appropriate for them at any particular time.[101]

The Tanzanian society he envisaged would be built on three fundamental principles, namely: equality, democracy and self-reliance. The first principle is threefold: social equality that is founded on the reason that 'a person-centered society has to promote the dignity and excellence of all human beings who are its members[102]; equality of all people guarantees their right to dignity that ensures the satisfaction of their basic necessities of life[103]; the right to dignity implies equal opportunities to the goods of this world, to education, and to service for the country, having in its background the attitude of mutual obligation and mutual respect;[104]economic equality that implies the absence of exploitation and a sharing of the fruits of the citizens' entire efforts; people's control of their means of production and exchange;[105]political equality that implies the right of all members of society to share in their own governance, equal

---

[99] Idem, *Tanzania Socialism-Ujamaa and Gaudium et Spes*, pp.6-7.

[100] Idem, *Ujamaa,* p.104; Idem, *Freedom and Socialism*, p.25.

[101] Idem, *Freedom and Socialism,* p.19; Idem, *Ujamaa,* p.92.

[102] Idem, *Freedom and Socialism*, pp.4-5.

[103] Idem, *Freedom and Unity,* p.15.

[104] Ibid.., *Freedon and Unity,* p.139; *Tanzania Socialism-Ujamaa and Gaudium et Spes*, p.16.;

[105] Idem, *Freedom and Socialism*, p.305; Idem, *Tanzanaian Socialsim- Ujamaa and Gaudium et Spes*, p.17.

sovereignty and ability to exert their sovereignty within the limits of law and constitutional framework of their society.[106]

The second principle of democracy is essentially related to the principle of equality. Nyerere hoped to build a democratic Tanzanian society that would have four essential features: "a closely united society in which no severe divisions existed to produce a demand for rival political parties; there would be a single national movement open to all citizens and committed to the promotion of the common good; there would be a Sovereign National Assembly whose members would be periodically and freely elected by all citizens; within that National Assembly, there would be as full an approximation as possible to the government by discussion."[107]

Nyerere considered democracy in the African traditional tribal methods of conducting affairs whereby the elders sat under a tree and talked until they agreed.[108]This understanding of democracy needed modification so that it could suit the new conditions of Tanzania by freely elected representatives of people meeting in parliament on behalf of their fellow citizens. Such democratic participation certainly would serve as an African contribution to the dynamic concept of democracy.

The third principle of self-reliance is established on Nyerere's conviction that the development of Tanzania can first depend on the Tanzanians themselves. He says: "There is no choice for us.

---

[106] Idem, *Freedom and Socialism,* p.5; Idem, *Tanzanian Socialism-Ujamaa and Gaudium et Spes,* p.17.
[107] C.Pratt, *The Critical Phase in Tanzania 1945-1968: Nyerere and the Emergency of Socialist Strategy,* London: Cambridge University Press, 1976, p.70; Idem, *Tanzanian Socialism-Ujamaa,* p.20.
[108]Idem, *Freedom and Unity*, p.195).

We shall be thankful for any outside assistance we receive, but we must not expect it. The only people we can rely upon are ourselves."[109] Furthermore, 'Tanzania can achieve political independence if her citizens can control the means by which they earn their living.[110]On this account, "independence should mean self-reliance."[111]

This implies that 'Tanzanians must make maximum of the resources they have. They must make their policies and control their country. The application of the principles of efficiency and professional experience is crucial in the processes of achieving developmental objectives.[112] According to Nyerere, foreign aid is welcome and appreciated in so far as it can help the people themselves and their country according to the objectives they have set for themselves.[113]

In short, The Tanzania Mwalimu Nyerere envisaged would develop along the path of self-reliance. This would be achieved by 'the Tanzanians through their efforts and by the use of the natural resources. Foreign assistance would only help in subsidizing the local efforts to speed up the process.'[114]

There is no doubt that Mwalimu Nyerere's vision for the Tanzanians provided a bonding principle for and among them. It cemented the people together regardless of their tribes, races, languages, social status and religions. Unfortunately, the centralization of political power, decision making processes and

---

[109]Idem, *Freedom and Socialism*, p.167.
[110]Idem, *Freedom and Development,* p.218.
[111]Idem, *Ujamaa,* p.23.
[112]Idem, *Tanzanaian Socialism-Ujamaa*, p.22.
[113]Ibid.., pp22-23; Idem, *Freedom and Socialism,* pp.386-388.
[114]Idem, *Tanzanian Socialism-Ujamaa*, p.26.

economic planning did not prioritize and enhance the basic foundation of equality, democratic participation and promotion of self-reliance.

Likewise the administrative structures and policies were hardly inspired by the values of "Ujamaa" (familyhood) ideal, namely: equality, solidarity, subsidiarity and the common good. The inner motivation to work for the common good did not guide the practical application and behaviour of Tanzanians at all levels in their daily life as they executed their basic social, political and economic duties.

Mwalimu Nyerere participating in activities of building better houses (Source: MNF Archive)

Even when in the mid 80's Tanzania made a major shift in policy from "Ujamaa" system to the liberal capitalistic system, the social behaviour never changed. The fundamental reason is that the motivation driven by the virtuous spirit to work for the common good, to give each person his/her basic rights and ask from each person their basic socio-political, economic and spiritual duties never changed.

It is therefore, not systems that will lead Tanzanians to achieve their developmental goals in the eradication of abject poverty, ignorance and communicable diseases; but moral motivation to work for the common good of all people regardless of their differences of tribe, race, gender, social status and religion.

In spite of these and many other challenges that Mwalimu Nyerere's egalitarian approach to development of Tanzania faced, his vision did not completely fail. Probably it was the best choice for the improvement of the conditions of the peasant masses of Tanzania. Tanzanians now can regard themselves as persons with something to share with other people world over. Moreover, out of the developmental adventures and related challenges, they know that Tanzania can only be developed by the people themselves. Other people can only help them to realize their sustainable development through this long process.[115]

The challenges faced during the 24 years of Mwalimu Nyerere's leadership tenure may not be the basis for ignoring or disregarding the principles he believed in and articulated with passion. Tanzanians can learn from the aims as well as the challenges related to the implementation of the vision of the Tanzania he had at heart. In this way draw an objective action-oriented recommendations for the direction they want to take towards the people-oriented development within the prevailing circumstances.

---

[115]Idem, *Tanzania Socialism-Ujamaa,* pp.27-33; *Hotuba ya Rais Julius Kambarage Nyerere Katika Bunge,* Dar es Salaam, 29 Julai 1985.

4
CHAPTER

MWALIMU NYERERE'S VISION OF EDUCATION

Mwalimu Julius Kambarage Nyerere's vision of education gradually developed throughout his formative years. Mwalimu Nyerere had a desire to improve the lives of others. He gradually carried out this motive all through his studies and later on during his political leadership. His vision of education developed within the basic orientation and life view for application in the service of sustainable development of the peasant masses of Tanzania.

Mwalimu Nyerere's vision of education developed from an attempt to think seriously about the question: "What is the education system in Tanzania intended to do – what is its purpose?"[116]An adequate response to this question develops from his vision of the post-independence Tanzanian society he envisaged. As it was discussed in chapter two, it is a society which is based on three principles: 'equality and respect for human dignity; sharing of resources which were produced by the people's efforts; work by everyone and exploitation by none'.[117]

Therefore, the Tanzania education system has to "foster the social goals of living together, for the common good. It has to prepare our young people to play a dynamic and constructive part in the development of the society in which all members share fairly in

---

[116] Idem, Education for Self-Reliance: Policy Document, March 1967, in Nyerere on Education, Dar es Salaam, HakiElimu, 2004, p.71.
[117] Ibid.

the good or bad fortune of the group, and in which progress is measured in terms of human well-being, not prestige, buildings, cars, or other things, whether privately or publicly owned [...] education must therefore inculcate a sense of commitment to the total community, and help the pupils to accept the values appropriate to [....]kind of future, not those appropriate to [....] colonial past."[118]

It means that the Tanzanian education system must 'emphasize cooperative endeavour, not individual advancement; stress concepts of equality and responsibility, giving service which goes with any special ability; and counteract the temptation to intellectual arrogance which leads the well-educated to disregard those whose abilities are non-academic but are just human beings'.[119] Such education should prepare young people for the work they will be called upon to do in a largely rural society. It has to prepare them to think for themselves and draw judgements regarding the issues affecting the people; moreover, interpret the decisions made democratically through societal institutions; and implement them within the prevailing circumstances.[120]

Therefore, the education that is conducive to an egalitarian society must focus on developing in every citizen three things, namely: "an enquiring mind; an ability to learn from what others do, and reject or adapt it to his (her) own needs; and a basic confidence in his (her) own position as a free and equal member of the society, who values others and is valued by them for what he (she) does and not for what he (she) obtains".[121]

---

[118]Idem, p.72.
[119]Ibid.., pp.72-73.
[120]Ibid.., p.73.
[121]Ibid.

Consequently, primary education has to be complete in itself. It must prepare primary school children for the life which the majority of them will lead. Conversely, the education provided in primary school should not be merely a preparation for entry to secondary schools, since we are aware of the fact that the majority of children would not go to those schools. Likewise, secondary school education must prepare young people for life and service for the general development primarily required for the rural peasant masses as well as the nation.

On the other hand, the purpose of secondary school education should not primarily focus on the preparation of young people for joining the university or other institutions of higher learning. This implies that the type of education given at the two levels (primary and secondary) must focus on the knowledge, skills, values and attitudes to be acquired and cherished with a view of contributing to the improvement of the people's lives in rural areas and the nation as a whole.[122]

Above all, university education anywhere in the world, and more so in the developing nation of Tanzania, has to focus on a scientific and objective examination of the facts and conditions under which the majority of Tanzanians live. These include: the poverty, the ignorance, the disease, the social attitudes, and the political atmosphere. The facts found by this scientific and objective approach should be used to design practical actions for making fundamental changes in the miserable conditions under which the people live and further their sustainable development.[123]

---

[122]Ibid., pp.79-81; Idem, Musoma Resolution: Directive on the Implementation of "Education for Self-Reliance", Musoma, November 1974.

[123]Idem, Nyerere on Education, "University, an Investment of the Poor in Their Own Future", Opening of the University College Campus, Dar es Salaam, 21 August, 1964.

This is only possible if it fulfills its three major functions, namely: transmitting advanced knowledge as a basis of further research and action; advancing the frontiers of knowledge for the development of people and entire human society; developing high-level academic knowledge, practical skills, social attitudes and beliefs necessary for maximum service to the development priorities of the present and the future society of Tanzania.[124]

Adult education forms an integral and essential part of Mwalimu Nyerere's vision of education in the service of the people-centered development, especially in the developing countries like Tanzania. This is born of his firm conviction that people can develop themselves as individuals and communities together. This is entrenched in his understanding of the purpose of education.

Mwalimu Julius K. Nyerere teaching elder women how to read and write during implementation of Adult Education program in one school (Source: MNF Archives).

---

[124]Idem, Inauguration of Dar es Salaam University, Dar es Salaam, 29 August 1970.

According to Mwalimu Nyerere, the purpose of education is the 'liberation of the human person from the restraints and limitations of ignorance and dependency. Education has to increase the persons' physical and mental freedom, increasing their control over themselves, their own lives and their environment. The ideas and skills imparted by education should contribute to their liberation. Education should help them, as individuals and in cooperation with their fellow men and women, to think clearly; examine alternative courses of actions; make choices between those alternatives bearing in mind their own purposes; and enable them to translate and implement the decisions drawn there from'.[125]

Consequently, education for liberation is for cooperation among people with the end in view of liberating themselves from the constraints of nature and fellow men and women. It is, therefore, a reality of great social significance, for the people whom education liberates are in society, which is ultimately affected by the changes brought about by education. Adult education should promote change in men and women as well as in the entire society, building upon what is already in existence. Adult education is, therefore, key to the development of free men and women and free societies, helping them to think, make their decisions, and execute them for their sustainable development.[126]

Therefore, 'the primary function of Adult education is to arouse a desire for change inspired by a conviction that there is need for change; and that change is possible. People living in poverty,

---

[125]Idem, "Adult Education and Development", Opening Speech to the International Adult Education Conference, Dar es Salaam, 21 June 1976.

[126]Ibid.

disease and exploitation are empowered to recognize that they can move out of these miseries by their own actions, individually and in cooperation with others. Secondly, Adult education should help people to work out the kind of change they want, and how they want to achieve it. Therefore, Adult education is the vital source and force for developing a free people who are empowered to determine their own future'.[127]

4.1 Implementation

The implementation of Mwalimu Julius Kambarage Nyerere's vision of education for an egalitarian Tanzanian society has shown mixed results. No doubt the vision provided a binding force for the nation. It bound together the Tanzanians despite their tribal, racial, linguistic and religious differences. Adult illiteracy has largely been overcome. The expanded primary school system has enabled almost all children at the age of seven to go to school. Many young people have gone to secondary, university and other tertiary educational institutions.[128] But to a greater extent the educational system, at all levels, namely: Primary, Secondary, University and other tertiary educational institutions, has not been adequate enough in responding to and fulfilling the aspirations of Tanzanians as described in the Education for Self-Reliance policy document of 1967.

As we have seen earlier on, Primary education was to be complete. It was meant to prepare pupils for the life of the village which the majority of them will lead. It was, therefore, needed to be good, sufficient and directly relevant to the ability of the children to be productive and participating members of a free and

---

[127]Ibid.

[128]Idem, "The Situation and Challenges of Education in Tanzania", Education Seminar, Arusha, 22 October 1984.

developing egalitarian society. It was to provide them with basic reading, writing and communication skills; techniques of doing things, based on the knowledge of local and national resources; basic skills relevant to a better life in villages and towns.[129] Primary education was to have Adult education, and centers for technical and craft training as supplement, meant for increasing and improving the young people's skills in agriculture, book keeping, carpentry, mechanics, or in any other useful technical skills for their individual, community, societal and national development.[130]

Likewise, Secondary education was meant for the provision of a 'reservoir' of young people with technical knowledge. This included teachers, health workers, engineers, mechanics, and administrators. These were to be recruited for the specialized services to the people in the rural areas and towns. The challenges which faced the implementation were similar to those that faced the implementation of primary education.

The need for specialized technical education was also emphasized with the view of accelerating economic development. Preparations were undertaken and directives for implementation were given by the Government and the National Executive Committee was to foresee the immediate exercise. Unfortunately, the intended objectives of preparing young people – men and women – for self-reliance; and enabling the schools to earn income for self-sustainability remained a dream that could not become true.

Above all, university and technical tertiary institutions education was meant for producing highly educated and skilled women and

---

[129]Ibid.
[130]Ibid.

men. These were to contribute in the transformation of the majority of Tanzanians' life from abject poverty, curable diseases and unwarranted ignorance to decent dignified life. Their acquired knowledge and skills was supposed to enable them to become committed members of their society, in service of their sustainable development. University and technical tertiary education was supposed to promote confidence in the graduates, develop a spirit of committed selfless service, willingness and creative and innovative ability of working together with others for the common good of Tanzanians.

Mwalimu Nyerere recognized the fact that "the process of changing completely an established system of education necessarily takes a long time before seeing the results, regardless of the substantial changes in the syllabus to reflect the Tanzanian objective conditions and national policy of Education for Self-Reliance. Moreover, the Tanzanians' mentality has not been liberated from the thinking that our students can be educated properly and graduate by the proposed system with the qualifications which meet the threshold of international standards. Likewise, the notable failure to transform schools into becoming part of economic set up by being productive through agriculture and other means is evident. Moreover, the employment policies have not included in the criteria of suitable candidates for recruitment such aspects as commitment, general behaviour, societal attitudes and values, working for the common good or another qualities."[131]

---

[131]Idem, "Musoma Resolution: Directive on the Implementation of Education for Self-Reliance", Musoma, November 1974.

4.2 Challenges

4.2.1 Transformation of Attitudes

The purpose of education, at all levels (primary, secondary, university, tertiary technical institutions) should be the provision of complete education empowering young men and women with knowledge and attitudes for the general development of the Tanzanians, especially the peasant rural masses. Secondly, all students in schools should participate in communal productive activities as an essential and integral part of their training. Therefore, there was need to restructure the examinations for establishing a combined assessment of the students' theoretical and practical productive work for the school and the village communities.[132]

Unfortunately, substantial changes in the current education system have hardly succeeded in forming attitudes and self-confidence necessary for eradication of poverty, ignorance and disease in Tanzania. Likewise, the system has not succeeded in making the students appreciate their obligation of being productive through agriculture and other self-reliance activities to reduce the government's financial burden in running the academic schools and institutions of higher learning, thus contribute to the productive work for the rural communities' sustainable development.[133] Furthermore, the majority of Tanzanians have failed to acknowledge the fact that the young people who are not selected for secondary or university education have successfully

---

[132] Idem, "Musoma Resolution: Directive on the Implementation of Education for Self-reliance", Musoma, November 1974; Idem, "The Situation and Challenges of Education in Tanzania", Education Seminar, Arusha, 22 October, 1984.
[133] Ibid

completed their primary education rather than considering them as total 'failures".[134]

4.2.2 Expansion of Primary Education

The people's response to the call to live in planned villages came about with the need of more primary schools to ensure places for all children of school age in these villages. The successful response to this need require very careful planning of the provisions of many qualified teachers, new teaching methods, teaching materials and substantial government funding. The alternative ways for achieving the same objectives, such as: using the same classrooms for morning and afternoon classes; using some secondary school students to teach lower classes for the provision of increased demand for more teachers did not meet the objective standards for the attainment of Universal Primary Education.[135]

4.2.3 Expansion of Secondary Education

The underlying need for expansion of Secondary School Education was to provide human power for sustainable development of Tanzanians. On this assumption Forms V and VI were introduced in secondary schools to prepare students for university education. The implementation of this plan faced more or less similar challenges as earlier on discussed regarding the expansion of Primary school education. More and well trained teachers other than using students of higher forms remained a perennial need; more classrooms were required; overhauling the existing system and practice became unachievable ideal.[136]

---

[134] Ibid
[135] Ibid.
[136] Ibid

4.2.4 Specialised Technical Education

Greater emphasis was to be placed on scientific and technical education. The main purpose was to prepare young men and women for self-reliance, for national development, and for the schools to earn some income for their sustainability. Thus a two year course in technical education for standard seven leavers, particularly those who did not secure admission in secondary schools or other training institutions, was introduced. These were meant for 'training in technical skills, agriculture, animal husbandry, commerce, home economics and accountancy'.[137]There is therefore hardly substantive evidence for the fulfillment of the intended results as originally directed. The challenges towards the realization of this objective include transformation of attitudes related to aspiration to university education and consequent white collar jobs and good life. The belief that technical education could help them to satisfy their needs remained too farfetched.

4.2.5 Adult education challenges

According to Mwalimu Nyerere, adult education enables people to know the ability they have to take action in changing the conditions, which entangles them in the circle of poverty, disease and ignorance. Secondly, it empowers them with the knowledge, skills and methods regarding working together to improve the conditions in which they live. Thirdly, it builds their understanding of the plans for nation economic development and the need for them to participate in the successful realization of these plans for the common good in the society. In a nutshell, adult education is about learning everything that helps all

---

[137]Ibid.

members of the society to understand environment they live in and the manner in which they can use and change it in order to improve their lives. Adult education applies to every member of the society, without exception.

These noble goals were not realized due to the unpreparedness of the teachers for it. In most cases they were satisfied with lucrative results of reading and writing skills which their clients acquired regardless of helping them to work out their development. The relevance of this achievement and its empowerment engagements was not given reasonable attention. The learners' attitudes remained as they were before; the vicious circles of poverty, ignorance and disease remained if not worsened.

4.2.6 University Education

Changes in the university entry requirements were introduced. It was no longer the applicants' Form VI examinations results only. Other factors to be considered, such as: good character, attitudes, industriousness, and service spirit, were to be given serious consideration. The implementation of this scheme faced some problems, like: shortage of students to fill the available places at the university; the high cost of educating students that included board and logging; full salary paid by government to the students who were public servants in government organs, among others.[138]

4.2.7 Work and Education in Education Institutions

Work and related production processes were to become an integral part of normal routine of students' learning activities, especially in secondary and tertiary institutions. The persistent wrong attitudes among parents, teachers and government officials

---

[138]Ibid.

that work was incompatible with studies stifled the entire implementation of the intended integration of studies and production processes. Unfortunately, a more fundamental purpose of making work and integral part of education, namely: developing an inner motivation of every Tanzanian, at different levels, to work for the common good was missed out.[139]

4.2.8 Examinations

The examination system, as it were, is meant to measure the students' level of understanding what has been taught. It is logical that if the objective of education was to develop in the learners the ability to become people who would contribute to the development of their fellow Tanzanians, then a new examination system was to be established. Therefore, a new examination structure that was meant to measure both the students' progress in the classroom and the productive work out of class that forms part of their education was to be designed for determining the learners' performance.[140] Unfortunately this did not happen.

The critical areas discussed above were major challenging factors in the implementation of Mwalimu Nyerere's vision of education for the Tanzanians in search for sustainable development in freedom and equality. These challenges have continued to make education inadequate for the realization of the Tanzanians' developmental aspirations. At all levels (primary, secondary, university and all other tertiary institutions) the education system has failed to transmit the basic attitudes and basic relevant skills for a better life in Tanzanian villages and towns. It has failed to promote creativity, the ability to think critically, basic self-reliance skills for productivity, and societal attitudes and values of

---

[139]Ibid.
[140]Ibid.

equality, solidarity, and common good in the communities within which they are situated; and enhancing school-community linkages.

4.2.9 Liberal Capitalism and Nyerere's Education Vision

The liberal capitalistic policies of the mid-1980s created contradictions and changes in the Mwalimu Nyerere's education vision of the late 60s – early 70s. The liberal capitalistic policies focused on creating opportunities for the availability of more money. Nevertheless they hardly considered better foundations for every person to be respected, people's mutual caring, societal attitudes, values, and working in collaboration for the common good.

The liberal capitalistic vision of education focused on knowledge acquisition by memorizing the facts for passing examinations, thus qualify for higher education level or enter formal labour market contrary to Mwalimu Nyerere's vision of education for self-reliance and sustainable development of all Tanzanians. In fact this education paradigm shift continues to widen the gap among Tanzanians. Its focus is not any longer the development of critical mind and critical thinking for better knowledge acquisition, skills, values and attitudes for a better life in the town communities and the predominantly peasant society of Tanzania.

Consequently, over 50% of the young people cannot make it through such screening process by passing examinations at any given level of education (primary, secondary, tertiary). These form the youth group of the so called "failed" who eventually flock in towns and cities for the employment they can hardly secure for lack of needed creative skills and competencies.

Furthermore, the current education system discarded the enabling schools-communities learning-working relationship as Mwalimu Nyerere vision of education had envisaged and laboured to implement throughout the 1970s and early 1980s. In fact this learning-working network has been considered as a waste of time and valueless. The outcome is not praiseworthy; the graduates from the liberalized education system have hardly achieved creative knowledge, appropriate entrepreneurial skills, social values, attitudes, competencies and nationhood spirit necessary for the realization of sustainable development of the Tanzanians. The current education system hardly produces graduates who are well prepared to adequately deal with the Tanzanian developmental challenges of today and the near future for liberation and self-reliance, above all, the realization of the Tanzanian Development Vision (TDV) by 2025. Moreover, it has contributed to the youth's negative attitude towards agriculture and community life in the rural setting that provide immensely to the livelihood of the Tanzanians absolute majority and economy of the country.[141]

Mwalimu Nyerere's vision of education – Education for Self-Reliance – as the proper system of education for preparing young people to actively participate in their sustainable development is supported by prominent education research for social change scholars. For example, Freires, P., (1970) argues that 'any attempt to construct a theory of action must involve a serious and sincere

---

[141]For a detailed discussion see Ahmad, A.K., Krogh,E.,Gjotterud, "Reconsidering the Philosophy of Education for Self-Reliance (ESR) from an Experiential Learning Perspective in Contemporary Education in Tanzania", Education Research Change (ERSC), Vol.3 No.1, April 2014, Nelson Mandela Metropolitan University, Port Elizabeth, South Africa, pp.7-10).

attempt to understand the realities of daily lives'[142]Likewise, Kolbs, D.A. (1984) argues from the experiential learning point of view that all learning begins with concrete experience that forms basis for new concrete experiences or actions originating from a new understanding.

On this account, Mwalimu Nyerere's vision of education cannot be dismissed in the overall discourse of rethinking the education that is for liberation and service to the common good of Tanzanians. The arguments centred on failure in its implementation do not diminish its valuable contribution to the development agenda of all Tanzanians and their nation. Prominent education research for social change scholars have demonstrated the significant potential of Mwalimu Nyerere's vision of education in producing innovative and creative young Tanzanians empowered with positive attitudes and competencies to liberate Tanzanians from abject poverty, conquerable ignorance and curable diseases. Engagement in such education system will, to a greater extent, serve as an adequate and reasonable solution to the 'rural-urban migration of young people that result in social dislocation and in increased crime both in rural and urban areas'.[143]

The overall discourse of rethinking Mwalimu Nyerere's education vision - Education for Self-Reliance and Liberation – is supported by various scholars. For instance, Kadenyi, M. & Kariuki, M. (2011) examine the relevance and contribution of ESR in rethinking education for liberation and self-reliance for the realization of sustainable development in Tanzania and beyond.

---

[142]http://www.theeducationist.info/paulo-freire-pedagogy-oppressed-book-summary.

[143]Idem, p.10.

Kyaruzi, A.A., Gjotterud, S. & Krogh,E. (2014) argue the case for the need of revitalizing and supporting sustainable ESR as realistic means towards the realization of the Tanzania Development Vision (TDV) by 2025.[144]

Krogh, E and Jolly, L. (2012) discusses the power which this learning process has in 'stimulating the learners to become active participants in sustainable development that is dependent on who will and can act for change'. The fundamental question they raise regarding the answer to 'fostering hope, courage, tenacity, patience, perseverance, purposeful relationship among people and their environment, critical sense of judgment, are examples of the essential qualities which are at the heart of Mwalimu Nyerere's Education for Self-Reliance.[145]

The above selected studies, among many, serve as evidence for arguing a strong case for revisiting and revitalizing Mwalimu Nyerere's Education for Self-Reliance for Tanzania's sustainable development.

---

[144]See Education Research for Social Change (ERSC) Volume 3 No.1, April 2014, pp.3-19.
[145]Wals, A.E.J & Corcoran, P.B. (Eds.), Learning for Sustainability in times of accelerating changes, (pp.213-224):
http://www.wageningenacademic.com/learn4-e 13.

5

CHAPTER

REVISITING MWALIMU NYERERE'S VISION OF EDUCATION

5.1 Recognizing the "Signs of the Times" in Tanzania Today

The Ujamaa Society as a "Sign of the Times"[146] in Tanzania Today

The Ujamaa (family hood) society that Mwalimu Nyerere envisaged, as discussed in chapter two, was to bring about a new awareness among the Tanzanians. It was to become a society where people care for each other's welfare. Its focus was to ensure human equality and dignity, values which could be assured through respect for human rights. It was to promote greater democratic participation of all Tanzanians in the affairs of their development. It was to promote greater awareness of the value of sharing the benefits of culture and the natural resources as those generated by the people's productive activities. It was to arouse in the Tanzanians a thirst for a full and free life worth of each person. It was to energize the hopes of a human extended family

---

[146] The expression "sign of the times" is drawn from the Catholic Church's Documents of the Second Vatican Council, Gaudium et Spes: The Pastoral Constitution of the Church in the Modern World that expresses her responsibility to examine the concrete situation in the world in the light of the Gospel, with a view of carrying out her mission of building a just society, where people can live in fraternity and work together for their common good.

hood which optimistically aspires for a new humanity founded on the principles of truth, justice and fraternal love.[147]

Mwalimu Nyerere participating in better housing campaign at Magomeni houses (Source: MNF Archive).

Unfortunately, the ideals of Ujamaa have not been successfully implemented. This is the fact that Mwalimu Nyerere admitted in his retirement address to the Tanzanian National Parliament.[148] Undoubtedly, the Mwalimu Nyerere's vision of the Tanzanian society provided a binding force for the Tanzanians. It cemented people together despite their tribal, racial, religious, social, economic differences.

The centralization of political power, decision making and economic planning were not aligned with the basic foundations of equality, equal rights and opportunities for all Tanzanians as

---

[147]Rwelamira, J.B. (1988). Tanzanian Socialism – Ujamaa and Gaudium et Spes: Two Convergent Designs of Integral Human Development, p.93.
[148]Hotuba ya Rais Julius Kambarage Nyerere katika Bunge, Dar es Salaam, 29 Julai, 1985.

proclaimed by the Ujamaa philosophy. What existed as traditional structures and social groupings were integrated into one central organization. The government leaders limited democratic processes. The new socio-political and economic structures stifled the culture of participatory administration, moving from the Ujamaa values of equality, solidarity, common good and subsidiarity. These failures in the implementation of the Ujamaa ideals are fruits of the fact that the vision's moral motivation did not guide the practical applications and social behavior in daily life.

The major changes in policy from Ujamaa system to liberal capitalistic system in the mid 80's did not eradicate poverty, ignorance and disease in Tanzania. The failure is equally attributed to the lack of moral motivation to work for equality, solidarity, subsidiarity and the common good, the values of the Ujamaa vision. The illusive promise of making more money available for all Tanzanians has not assured sustainable development of all Tanzanians. Therefore, the validity of Ujamaa philosophy of building a society on the moral foundation where each person is respected, where people learn to take care of one another and the common good remains perennially valid in the processes for sustainable development.[149]

The context of Tanzania today remains a "sign of the times" in the sense that it provides and expresses the actual needs and aspirations of the Tanzanians. Likewise, it is a "sign of the times" for it provides an environment within which the Mwalimu Nyerere's vision of education is to become instrumental in building a better Tanzanian society that is founded on the values

---

[149]Missiaen, V., (07/10/2016). "50 Years Arusha Declaration", University of Edinburgh.

of dignity, equality, solidarity, truth, justice, peace, freedom, hard work and the common good.[150]

5.2 Mwalimu Nyerere's Education Vision and Tanzanian Ujamaa Society

Mwalimu Nyerere's education vision primary finality was to suit the developmental aspirations of the Tanzanians as specified in the Arusha Declaration (1967). His articulated finality of education remains valid. According to him, education should develop the learners' personality by stimulating their curiosity, creativity, initiative and incentive so that they can cope with concrete life situations. It has to develop in an individual a sense of personal integrity, social justice, love of God and neighbor. It should instill in an individual the values of social justice, human freedom and peace, leading individual persons to re-examine their attitudes, personal lives and actions. Moreover, it should create an awareness of social and moral evils existing in their family, community, and society, professional, economic, cultural, religious activities. Furthermore, education should aim at preparing the young people to choose a vocation for their life and for living this personal vocation in society with responsibility.[151]

5.3 Unity of Purpose for a New Ujamaa Society of Tanzania

The Tanzania Ujamaa society that Mwalimu Nyerere envisaged and labored to build was an ideal society that all Tanzanians were to participate in its realization. Tanzanians are still building up the culture and participatory structures towards the realization of the society in which the family hood spirit and the common good guide

---

[150]Idem, Tanzanian Socialism – Ujamaa, and Gaudium et Spes, pp.93-94.

[151]Ibid.., pp.105-107.

practical applications and every person's behavior in daily life. His education vision prioritizes the formation of a moral foundation where each person is respected, learns to care for one another and the common good, enjoys equal rights and their corresponding duties, the foundation of the general culture and basis for social behavior rooted in the values and principles to demand accountability from everyone including those entrusted with responsibilities for social, political, economic and administrative decision making.[152]

Unfortunately, there has not been sustained efforts in the ongoing formation of all Tanzanians in building a stronger foundation of values and moral principles and guidelines which must motivate them to embrace the unity of purpose in working for their sustainable development. Building a new society is still a work in progress. Changing from Ujamaa to liberal capitalism did not change the people's social behavior. Plans for sustainable development for a new Tanzania still fail for the same reasons, namely: lack of discipline, lack of sense of duty, poor participation in decision making processes, corruption, weak institutional capacity, poor and lack of control and monitoring of development planned programs.

Mwalimu Nyerere's vision of education has as its priority developing a moral foundation in service of unity of purpose in a new Tanzania where each person and all people learn to care for one another, and the common good. It is meant to develop a moral vision that ought to build the peoples' conviction that politics, wealth, resources and socio-political, economic, religious and administrative decision making services must be at the equitable service of all Tanzanians. Through initial and ongoing vision of education that focuses the developmental work guided by the principles of solidarity and subsidiarity, altruism, tolerance for social, political,

---

[152]Ibid.., Messien, Vic, 2016.

cultural and religious differences, honesty, sobriety, and courage in creativity, unity of purpose in venturing into building a new Ujamaa society of Tanzania by concerted efforts of every Tanzanian, can be achieved. These considerations lead us to explore the appropriate actions towards the revival of Mwalimu Nyerere's education vision for the formation of fundamental attitudes, convictions and practices in the process of building a new Ujamaa Tanzanian society.

6
CHAPTER

CONCRETE RECOMMENDATIONS

6.1 Education for Living

According to Mwalimu Nyerere, the whole approach to education which Tanzania has to provide at all levels – primary, secondary, tertiary – should empower the young and adult Tanzanians to live together and work together for their sustainable development. Mwalimu Nyerere tenaciously and repeatedly emphasized the two purposes of his education vision, namely:

> *"…to transmit from one generation to the next the accumulated traditional wisdom, knowledge and skills as well as scientific and technological skills in order to build a new a Tanzanian society. Secondly, it has to prepare people for their future membership of the society that is based on: human equality and respect for human dignity; equitable sharing of resources produced by the peoples' efforts; work together for the common good by everyone and exploitation by none".* [153]

---

[153]Idem, Address at the CHAKIWITA Symposium, Marangu Teachers' College, 12th September 1988. Idem, Education and Development in Africa: Second Michael Scott Memorial Lecture, Africa Education Trust, London, 4th June 1996; Idem, Education for Service and not Selfishness, on the occasion of the Award of an HONORARY Doctorate of Letters, The Open University of Tanzania, Dar es Salaam, 5 March 1988.

It is therefore evident that Mwalimu Nyerere's vision of education is indispensable for the cultivation and development of societal attitudes, values and virtues described earlier on, in the process of responding to the challenges of poverty, ignorance and disease. Moreover, it is essential for maintaining the major achievements resulting from the 50 years of its implementation. These include: provision of equitable access to education by female and male young and adult Tanzanians through universal primary education, primary, secondary and tertiary education programmes; enabling children and adults to value productive work as essential for their sustainability; promotion of human dignity, equality, mutual respect and unity among Tanzanians; production of human resources for the low and middle level administrative posts as well as teachers, medical doctors, engineers, technicians and scientists of numerous categories, government and religious leaders, politicians, professionals of various categories, internationally reputable scholars in international institutions and organizations.[154]

Likewise the very education vision has a great potential to instill in the younger generation of Tanzanians at all levels – primary, secondary, tertiary – curiosity, initiative and creativity; inner motivation to work for justice, dignity and equality, solidarity, subsidiarity and the common good within their respective institutions of learning; and later on within their social, political, economic, cultural and religious engagements. Such a spirit and attitude will build in them the strong spiritual and moral foundation to contribute in deepening the spirit of dedication to work, overcoming the vice of indifference to reasonable productivity, applying justice and equity in the distribution of

---

[154]Cf. Mosha, H.J., Twenty Years after Education for Self-Reliance: A Critical Review, Journal of Educational Development, Vol. 10, No.1, pp.65-66.

goods and services, and counteracting pronounced acquisitive drive and related vices. In this way education will be a strong and adequate force in achieving sustainable developmental aspirations of the Tanzanians, thus serve as a power of creative living in concrete life situations of a new Tanzanian Ujamaa society.[155]

It is therefore important for all partners in the provision of education – public and private – to collaborate in making adequate reforms towards the realization of "education for living". Such reforms need to start with

> *"...the attitudes and expectations which support the narrowly conceived idea that the objective of education is paid employment. This mentality has led many young people into professions in which they had no interest or practical experience, The basic criteria [....] being good examination results and academic degrees regardless of the candidates' general character, initiative, creativity, self-discipline, and suitability for such employment. This has contributed to the problems of inefficiency, mismanagement of public institutions, inadequate social services, irresponsibility, lack of discipline, and corruption. This mentality has become a great obstacle to achieving the type of education that should prepare people for living in a society whose fundamental aspirations are human dignity, greater equality and self-reliance.[156]*

These reflections lead us to discuss and propose actions to be taken in the processes of revitalizing the Tanzanian education

---

[155]Idem, Tanzanian Socialism – Ujamaa and Gaudium et Spes, pp.106-107; Idem, 50 Years Arusha Declaration.
[156]Ibid.., Tanzanian Socalism – Ujamaa, pp.107-108.

system for the realization of sustainable development of all people in Tanzania.

6.2 Action for Sustainable Development

Action for sustainable development of the Tanzanians ultimately depends on the vision of the Tanzanian society we envisage. As much as Mwalimu Nyerere's vision of Tanzania faced many challenges as discussed earlier on in chapter two, its validity still remains a force to reckon with. In fact its force lies in the foundational principles it propagates, namely: the dignity and equality of people, the need to protect the common good, involvement of every person in the life of the society inspired by the principle of subsidiarity, caring in solidarity and being responsible for one another. It affirms the conviction that the Tanzanian society would gradually achieve its sustainable development by the gradual conversion of the people's attitudes and the existing institutions through the determination of the Tanzanians' needs and taking the direction that is appropriate for them at any particular time.[157]

Mwalimu Nyerere argues a strong case for the validity of his education vision in the Second Michael Scott Memorial Lecture (4th June 1996) in affirmative terms:

In 1967[...], I issued a policy paper 'Education for Self-Reliance'. Regarding it.., I find that there is little if anything with which I can now disagree, but much that could be learned from the implementation (or for lack) of it. Its definition of the universal purpose of education

---

[157]Idem, Freedom and Socialism, p.19; Idem, Ujamaa: Essays on Socialism, pp.11 and 104; Idem, Tanzanian Socialism – Ujamaa and Gaudium et Spes, pp.6-7.

remains valid I think: "to transmit from one generation to the next the accumulated wisdom and knowledge of the society, and to prepare the young people for their future membership of the society and their active participation in its maintenance or development." The document also calls for the education given to be relevant to the society in which it takes place – currently and in the expected future. That too I think remains valid. 'Education for Self-Reliance' was issued in 1967 in the context of our aspiration to build socialism in Tanzania. In different countries or different times, 'relevant policies' might well be different from those of Tanzania at that time. That would certainly be true in a society going through a process of rapid change from an economic system based on the principles of cooperation [....] to an economic system based on individualism. And when social change results from external economic or political pressures [....] governments are [....] deliberately to face up to the social policy implications of what is happening.[158]

Learning from the above affirmation that is also supported by various scholars[159] one cannot underestimate or ignore the potential of Mwalimu Nyerere's vision of education for contributing to the development of the Tanzanian society and adequately responding to its developmental challenges. On this ground I propose a reconsideration of his vision in the current context of Tanzania. This exercise will include: the vision of the Tanzanian society today - (a reality that is not clearly defined at

---

[158]"Education and Development in Africa", Africa Today and Tomorrow, Dar es Salaam, Mwalimu Nyerere Foundation, 2000, Second Edition, pp.43-44.
[159]Cf. Kadenyi, M. and Kariuki, M. (2011); Krogh, E. and Jolly, L.(2012); Ahmad, A.K., Krogh, E. and Gjotterud, S.G. (2014).

present), the education policy to guide this vision and the process to guide the policy formulation for its implementation.

6.3 The Current Vision of Tanzanian Society

Chapter two has discussed the Tanzanian society Mwalimu Nyerere had envisaged and committed to develop. In a nutshell, it is a society that would grow and achieve its sustainable development by the gradual conversion of the people's attitudes and existing institutions. It would be built on three fundamental principles: equality, democracy and self-reliance. It would be inspired by the Ujamaa values of equality, solidarity, subsidiarity, and the common good. Unfortunately these principles and values have not satisfactorily guided the practical application and behavior of Tanzanians at all levels in their daily life as they executed their basic social, political, economic and spiritual responsibilities. The shift in policy from Ujamaa paradigm of development to the liberal capitalistic one in the mid 80's to date, hardly contributed to the inner motivation of Tanzanians at different levels to work for the common good, thus achieve their developmental goals in eradicating poverty, ignorance and disease.

It is important to note that despite the many challenges Mwalimu Nyerere's egalitarian approach of development of Tanzanian society faced, it was probably the best choice for the improvement of the living conditions of many Tanzanians. Likewise, with review and adaptation to the new conditions, it remains a paradigm worth the energy in all the processes for sustainable development of the people and the nation of Tanzania.

From these perspectives, there is need to draw action-oriented recommendations for the direction Tanzania wants to take towards the people-oriented development within the prevailing circumstances. Therefore, we need to revisit the vision of the Tanzania we desire to build, the policy of education to guide and form the people for its realization, the process and key elements to guide the policy formulation and its implementation.

6.4 Revisiting the Vision of Tanzanian Society

There is an urgent need to reconsider the Tanzanian society we want to become and contribute to its developmental sustainability. I believe the Ujamaa Tanzanian society Mwalimu Nyerere had envisaged remains an ideal and a guiding goal for the nation and its people. It is convincing to devote time, energy and resources to build such a society for the values it cherishes, namely: love, compassion, self-discipline, generosity, truthfulness, respect, justice, unity, peaceful coexistence; and its guiding principles of: human dignity and equality, protection of the common good, involvement of every member in its life by following the principle of subsidiarity, care for one another in solidarity within the social, political, economic, religious everyday life experiences of the Tanzanians and ever changing realities of Tanzanian society.

In order to work fruitfully for the realization of her revised vision, Tanzania needs innovative and creative young and adult citizens who are empowered with knowledge, skills, competencies, attitudes, values and moral motivation by the education that is tailored for this end. This calls for the education policy that is designed to serve the vision of Tanzanian society described earlier on.

6.5 Revisiting Tanzania Education Policy

The process needs to begin with a scientific assessment of the merits and weaknesses of the Education for Self-Reliance (ESR) policy that has guided Tanzania and her people to realize the major developmental achievements described earlier on. The principle to subsidiarity ought to guide such a noble process; all stakeholders have to be involved. These include parents and guardians, students, academicians, technocrats and business communities, politicians, political parties, the Ministry of Education and various relevant government ministries, and religious bodies. Information has to be collected, open debates be conducted in view of identifying the policy goals, implementation means, especially budgetary allocations, foreseen implementation challenges. The climax of the process ought to be a clear interpretation of facts within the prevailing conditions of the Tanzanians. It is equally crucial to describe the roles of each stakeholder in the policy implementation processes, namely: parents and guardians associations, students and youth associations, teachers and academicians, members of political parties, trade unions, religious associations and employers in view of effective and successful policy implementation.[160]

6.6 Life Values-Centered Curriculum

Curriculum development and implementation should focus on developing and promoting the values which make society a truly human family/community. These include: trust, solidarity, altruism, companionship, honesty, generosity, respect of each one's dignity, acceptance of differences, forgiveness for wrong done, and giving wrong doers a new chance. It should also seek to promote in the learners the vision of societal life expressed in the foundational principles of: the dignity of the human person, the protection of the common good, involvement in the life of the

---

[160]Cf. Mosha, H.J. (1990), Twenty Years after Education for Self-Reliance: A Critical Review.

society by following the principle of subsidiarity, caring in solidarity for one another. The curriculum should focus on growing and enhancing the inner and moral motivation to work for the common good, to give each one basic rights and ask from each one basic social duties.

Therefore, each subject and content taught at any level of the education system in Tanzania, must not only seek learners to attain the goal of functional literacy that serves as a bridge to further education level. As much as this goal is important, nevertheless, the noblest goal should be to acquire the necessary skills and competencies, develop critical thinking with the view of making mature moral decisions essential for a sense of personal integrity, social justice, human freedom and peace necessary for sustainable life in the family, community and society in the new Tanzania.

These considerations will necessitate the change in the examination system. As discussed in chapter three, the current examination system focus on the reproduction of memorized facts, pass examination with good grades, qualify for higher education level, or secure job opportunity as unskilled worker. This system disregards elements of creativity, critical thinking, problem-solving skills, values, positive attitude towards work and other societal attitudes; and inner motivation for active and productive life in the community and society at large. It hardly tests how the imparted knowledge can be employed to solve the developmental challenges related to poverty, ignorance and disease thus becoming a real force for improving the living conditions of the people in their immediate communities and the nation as a whole.

Therefore, it is necessary to design a new system of examination that captures the student's progress in classroom/lecture hall and his/her performance in other work and functions that form an essential part of the education programme undertaken. Concretely, the students' progressive assessment should include understanding and assimilation of the facts taught in class/lecture hall, and the performance out of class/lecture hall regarding elements of creativity and innovation, critical thinking, positive attitudes towards work, active engagement in the community activities with the spirit of justice and solidarity in the realization of community projects in their specific social and economic circumstances. As Mwalimu Nyerere put it:

> *"...the student's progress in the classroom plus his (her) performance of other functions and the work which he (she) will do as part of his (her) education, must all be continually assessed and combined results is what constitutes his (her) success or failure"[161]*

6.7 Teacher Education

Life Values-Centered Curriculum can be implemented by teachers who are trained for this purpose. This is a wake-up call for the radical transformation in teachers' training programs, so that the graduates from the teachers training institutions can succeed in imparting to learners the knowledge, skills, competencies, principles and attitudes for sustainable

---

[161] Idem, "Musoma Resolution: Directive on the Implementation of "Education for Self-Reliance", Musoma, November 1974; this assessment approach is supported by socio-constructive learning perspective and experiential learning perspective scholars – cf. Idem, "Reconsidering the philosophy of Education for Self-Reliance (ESR) from an experiential learning perspective in contemporary education in Tanzania, April 2014, pp.3-19.

development of Tanzanians. Teachers' training should aim at the formation that aligns with the demands of the developmental needs of each and every member of the Tanzanian society. As it was pointed out earlier on, the planning process to achieve this ever-demanding goal has to engage all stakeholders: policy makers, Ministry of Education and relevant Government ministries, senior administrators, deans of education faculties, principals and educators of teachers training institutions.

The point of departure for the planning process should start with deeper analysis of essential aspects for teachers' training programs for accomplishment of desired learning outcomes. In this respect the focus should be on

> '...programs that can produce teachers who have the knowledge, skills, dispositions and commitment to assisting students to become responsible citizens of their communities and the Tanzanian society at large.'[162]

Teachers training curriculum should be innovative enough to include on its list of the courses to be taken: critical thinking, environment and its protection, peace and democracy in multi-parties context, respect for human dignity, the dignity of work, equality, solidarity, subsidiarity, responsible citizenship, justice and common good in the context of Tanzania society today and the foreseeable future.

The second consideration should be the review of institutional structures and resources that should support the teachers' transformative capacity building. This must include creating

---

[162]Cf. Chaudhary, P. (2014). "Rethinking Teacher Education for Liberating Learning", p.2730, Scholarly Research Journal, www.srjis.com; Cf. Idem, "The Situation and Challenges of Education in Tanzania", Education Seminar, Arusha, 22nd October 1984.

frameworks within which learners can actively participate in the planning and implementation of their community-based learning processes within and with the local communities where they are situated. The new systemic approach of teachers training can be implemented by the competent educators and administrators of teacher training institutions who should regularly undertake professional development programmes in order to effectively support and enhance the contextualized students' learning process for sustainable development of the Tanzanians and their nation. This Educational learning and training approach is supported by established socio-constructive learning and experiential learning study perspectives discussed earlier on.

6.8 Role of education regulators

Generally, the role of education regulators (Regulatory bodies/statutory educational bodies) is to promote quality by ensuring the standard required for specific levels of education are met. Moreover, they play supportive, constructive and advisory roles to improving the standards of teaching and quality learning; allowing new innovative approaches in the delivery of high quality education whose sole objectives is to drive the agenda of sustainable development.

Within the context of Mwalimu Nyerere's vision of education, there is a need for the reformation of the regulatory framework that is formative for job creators within the perspective of self-reliance. The main objectives/focus and criteria for high quality education ought to be the extent to which it arouses curiosity and provokes questioning, thus challenging old assumptions and established practices for the common good of Tanzanians.

According to Mwalimu Nyerere's vision, the quality of education provided has to be determined by its appropriateness to Tanzania's development needs.[163]. Innovative approaches in the delivery of education need to focus more on developing "enquiring minds and questioning approaches to techniques of things based on knowledge of local and national resources[164]. The major objectives for innovative approaches ought to be the formation of attitudes and self – confidence necessary for general development within the Tanzanian Development Vision (TDV) by 2025. Thus, resolve challenges related to abject poverty, conquerable ignorance and curable diseases.

6.9 Witness by Life-Style

Mwalimu Julius Kambarage Nyerere witnessed by his person and the life style the vision of education that he proposed. The 24 years of his total dedication in the service of the Tanzanians are marked with the faithful adherence to the principles he articulated in his vision of education. He lived by the principles of: equality and respect of human dignity. He served to foster the social goals of living together, and working together, for the common good. He wanted no privileges for himself and his family; he fought all forms of corruption, and was an example of not engaging in corrupt deals even when it would cost the country foreign aid. He worked with people in his Butiama rural home and different part of Tanzania in farms, planting, weeding, harvesting, making bricks with local people for their permanent residence houses.

---

[163] J.K Nyerere, Education seminar, Arusha 22nd October 1984.
[164] Ibid

As much as he was well-educated and Head of the State, he devoted his time to motivate the rural peasant communities and the elders to think for themselves, make judgments on all issues affecting them and implement their decisions in the light of their peculiar local circumstances. He exercised and realized his teaching responsibility as a perennial teacher, *"Mwalimu"* – an official title he preferred throughout his life and service as President of Tanzania – as he consistently encouraged the Tanzanians to develop in themselves and enquiring mind, an ability to learn from what others do, and reject or adapt it to their own needs. Moreover, he instilled in them a basic confidence to live as free and equal members of society, to value themselves and each other for who they are and not what they own.

Of course as a person, many at times, he would over-react when he was faced with disappointment related to the poor and not being more vigorous in the implementation of his will. Mwalimu Nyerere was well aware of the threat to his authority posed by the so-called "non-believers" – (leaders in the Government, Civil Service and even in the ruling Political Party) – who failed to show by actions that they cared for people and challenged creative Ujamaa management and administration system. He made mistakes; nevertheless he took courage to admit and change the policies in question to correct these mistakes for the good of the less fortunate masses of rural peasant farmers. As he put it:

> *"None of us is perfect. We cannot always see the full implications of what we do or say; and however much we try, none of us always resists the temptations of arrogance of office.*[165]

---

[165]Idem, Africa Today and Tomorrow, Dar es Salaam, (2000), p.24.

Indeed, by his exemplary life-style, he has managed to pave way for a united Tanzanian Ujamaa society at least during the 24 years of his dedicated service to the nation. He never got tired in propagating education for peace, unity and people-centred development in Africa because that was his belief:

"I am simply a believer, like many other believers, in the world and in human history. I believe in the equality and dignity of all human beings, and the duty to serve, their well-being as well as their freedom in a peaceful and co-operative society. I am an ardent believer in the freedom and welfare of the individual. [...].But I also believe that what gives humanity to our individuality, is a sense of community and fellowship with all other human beings wherever they may be."[166]

Thereafter his tenure as President of Tanzania, he continued to live work for the realization of the same principles and the values he held dear for peace, unity and people-centered development in Tanzania and Africa. As Chairman of the South Centre, Mwalimu said:

"I firmly believe that the future of Africa will be grim indeed if we do not try hard to promote those objectives: we need peace within nations and between nations. The inheritance of diversity is a blessing which we must preserve and promote. But it has to be the diversity of a basically united people and a basically united continent. [....] development which promotes peace and unity, is not a cause of strife and disunity

---

[166]Ibid., p.23. Cf. Idem, Hotuba ya Rais Julius K. Nyerere katika Bunge, Dar-es-Salaam, 29 Julai, 1985.

It is therefore an imperative for every Tanzanian to learn from the living example of Mwalimu Nyerere. If Tanzania has to achieve her developmental aspirations, every Tanzanian, more so, all categories of leaders in their various sections have to follow Mwalimu Nyerere's example. They should affirmatively explain and be living examples of abiding by the Education for Self-Reliance goals and objectives within the prevailing Tanzanian social, political, economic, cultural and religious context. Leaders of all categories must not be preachers regarding what is essential for the realization of Tanzania Development Vision (TDV) 2025. They ought to be practitioners whose life-style demonstrate the reality that values and principles described earlier on are worthy pursuing and abiding by for workable daily engagement in noble tasks for sustainable development of the Tanzanians and their nation.

6.10 Conclusion

The main objective of this study was to conduct a critical review of Mwalimu Julius Kambarage Nyerere's vision of education – Education for Self-Reliance (ESR) – and examine its relevance in driving the agenda of the people-centered development in the prevailing circumstances of Tanzania today and in the near future. We have reviewed the principles, social attitudes, skills and competencies it is meant to transmit to the entire citizenry of Tanzania for the realization of the people-centered development, founded on human dignity and equality, solidarity, truth, justice, peace, freedom, hard work and the common good.

---

[167]Idem, *Africa Today and Tomorrow*, pp.22-23.

Our examination of its implementation has shown mixed results. The vision has provided a binding force for the Tanzanians despite their tribal, racial, linguistic and religious differences. Adult illiteracy has been overcome; almost all children at the age of seven have gone to school; young people have gone to secondary, university and other tertiary educational institutions. Nevertheless, to a greater extent, the education system at all levels, has not been adequate enough in responding to the developmental aspirations of Tanzanians.

An in-depth discussion of the major challenges to the realization of ESR has been conducted. In summary, they include the failure to promote creativity, the ability to think critically, basic self-reliance skills and competencies for productivity; societal attitudes and values of equality, solidarity, and common good, enhancing school-community linkages; above all, the motivation to work for all these in the spirit of *Ujamaa* society that is founded on the principles of truth, justice, peace, sisterly and brotherly love within the matrix of shared responsibility.

In spite of these challenges, concrete recommendation have been made towards the realization of the major objectives of ESR in the process of its revitalization in the prevailing circumstances of Tanzania today and tomorrow. These recommendations seek to affirm the potential of ESR in guiding the processes for the realization of Tanzania Development Vision (TDV) 2025. It is an imperative for all leaders in Tanzania to become practitioners whose life style demonstrate the reality that values and principles have to be pursued and abided by for the workable daily engagement in noble tasks for people-centered development of the Tanzanians.

SELECTED BIOGRAPHIES

Atubonekisye, E.L.M.

He is currently Assistant Programmes Officer of the Mwalimu Nyerere Foundation. He offered special advice and technical support on the publication of this book.

Bache, V.G.

Cultural Heritage Management/Conservation Officer, Dar es Salaam, Tanzania.

Butiku, J.

He is the serving Executive Director and one of the founder Trustee of the Mwalimu Nyerere Foundation. In his long public career he has served as Principal/Private Secretary to President Julius K. Nyerere, the founding President of Tanzania during his administration. He also served as Principal/Private Secretary to President Ali Hassan Mwinyi.

Gallus, A.

He is currently Administrative Officer and Special Assistant to the Executive Director of the Mwalimu Nyerere Foundation — in his long service in the government he started as Court Clerk during colonial time, rose to Principal Secretary of various Ministries before he was promoted to become District and Regional Commissioner. He also served Chama cha Mapinduzi at different capacities.

Kabamanya, E.A.

Assistant Program Officer,

The Mwalimu Nyerere Foundation, Dar es Salaam, Tanzania.

Minael-Hossana, O. Mdundo

She is a retired Tanzania Army officer. She is the author of a book *"Masimulizi ya Sheikh Thabit Kombo Jecha."* She is a dedicated African Liberation historian.

Miraji, M.M.

Programmes Officer, the Mwalimu Nyerere Foundation, Dar es Salaam, Tanzania. He is also Secretary of the Tanzania National Committee for the Prevention of Genocide and Mass Atrocities.

Missiaen, V.

Born in Belgium in 1938. He is a member of the Missionaries of Africa Society (White Fathers). He was a member of the General Council of his Missionary Society in Rome (1974-1986). He has travelled widely in Africa; taught in Itaga Seminary, Tabora – Tanzania; served in the Parish of Chemchem, Catholic Diocese of Singida – Tanzania; worked for the Tanzania Episcopal Conference as Secretary to the Association of Religious Superiors; Secretary to the Justice and Peace commission; and to date Chaplain to the Christian Professionals of Tanzania.

REFERENCES

Ahmad, A.K., Krogh, E., Gjotterud, S.M. (2014). Reconsidering the Philosophy of Education for Self-Reliance (ESR) from an Experiential Learning Perspective in Contemporary Education in Tanzania. Education Research for Change, 3(1). Port Elizabeth: Nelson Mandela Metropolitan University.

Assey, J.J. (2014). Education for Self-Reliance Reconsidered. Pricard Printing Press.

Bwimbo, P.D.M. (2016). Mlinzi Mkuu wa Mwalimu Nyerere. Dar es Salaam. Mkuki na Nyota Publishers.

Freire, P. (1970). http:/www.theeducationist.info/paulo-freire-pedagogy-oppressed-book-summary.

Kadenyi, M., Kariuki, M. (2011). Rethinking Education for Liberation and Self-Reliance: An Examination of Nyerere's and Plato's Paradigm. International Journal of Curriculum and Instruction, 1(1).

Kolb, D.A. (1984). Experiential Learning. Engelwood Cliffs, USA: Prentice-Hall.

Krogh, E., Jolly, L. (2012). http://www.wageningenacademic.com/learn4-e.

Lema, E., Mbilinyi, M., Rajani, R. (Eds.). (2004). Nyerere on Education/Nyerere kuhusu Elimu. (Vols. I & II). Selected Essays and Speeches (1954-1998). Dar es Salaam: HakiElimu.

Molony, T. (2014). Nyerere: The Early Years. Woodbridge: Suffolk.

Mosha, H.J. (1990). Twenty Years after Education for Self-Reliance: Critical Review. International Journal of Educational Development, 10(1).

Mpangala, G.P, Mawazo, R.R. (2015). Historia ya Ukombozi: Mwalimu Julius Kambarage Nyerere. Dar es Salaam: TUKI.

Mwalimu Nyerere Foundation. (2000). Africa Today and Tomorrow. Dar es Salaam.

Nyerere, J.K. (1966). Freedom and Unity. London: Oxford University Press.

Nyerere, J.K. (1968). Freedom and Rural Development. London: Oxford University Press.

Nyerere, J.K. (1968). Ujamaa: Essays on Socialism. Dar es Salaam: Oxford University Press.

Nyerere, J.K. (1968). Freedom and Socialism/Uhuru na Ujamaa. Dar es Salaam: Oxford University Press.

Rwelamira, J.B. (1988). Tanzanian Socialism-Ujamaa and Gaudium et Spess: Two Convergent Designs of Integral Human Development. Roma: Academia Alfonsiana, Pontificia Universitas Lateranensis.

Vatican II. (1965). Gaudium et Spes – Pastoral Constitution on the Church in the Modern World. English translation in Austin Flannery, ed. Vatican II: The Conciliar and Post Conciliar Documents. Dublin: Dominican Publications, 1981 edition.

Willie, A.H. (2005). Recollections on President Julius Kambarage Nyerere. Unpublished Notes. Musoma.

www.ingramcontent.com/pod-product-compliance
Lightning Source LLC
Chambersburg PA
CBHW060446160726
47992CB00003B/1098